Basic Construction Management
The Superintendent's Job

Second Edition

Jerry Householder and Leon Rogers

Home Builder Press
National Association of Home Builders
15th and M Streets, N.W.
Washington, DC 20005

Basic Construction Management: The Superintendent's Job
ISBN: 0-86718-342-X

Library of Congress Cataloging in Publication Data

Householder, Jerry.
    Basic construction management, the superintendent's job / Jerry
Householder and Leon Rogers.—2nd ed.
        p.   cm.
    Rev. ed. of: Basic construction management, the superintendent's
job / Michael Eckert. © 1983.
    ISBN 0-86718-342-X : $20.00
    1. Building—Superintendence.   I. Rogers, Leon.   II. Eckert,
Michael. Basic construction management, the superintendent's job.
III. Title.
TH438.H67 1990   89-26681
690'.068—dc20   CIP

For further information, please contact:

Home Builder Bookstore
National Association of Home Builders
15th and M Streets, N.W.
Washington, D.C. 20005
(800) 368-5242

12/89 Monotype/Automated 5K

Contents

Acknowledgments

This publication was made possible through the cooperative efforts of many individuals. Special thanks to Bob Whitten for his careful review of the manuscript. Thanks are extended also to the Business Management Committee of NAHB and to Sonia Wilder of the Business Management Department.

This book was produced under the general direction of Kent Colton, NAHB Executive Vice President, in association with NAHB staff members James E. Johnson, Jr., Staff Vice President, Operations and Information Services; Adrienne Ash, Assistant Staff Vice President, Publishing Services; Curt Hane, Project Editor, and David Rhodes, Art Director.

About the Authors

Jerry Householder, builder, professor, and author, has many years of experience as a general contractor. Currently the Director of Graduate Studies in Construction Management in the College of Architecture and Urban Studies at Virginia Polytechnic Institute, Dr. Householder teaches courses in planning and scheduling, construction management, and construction law. A professor for ten years, the author holds a Ph.D in civil engineering from the Georgia Institute of Technology.

Jerry Householder is the author of NAHB's *Scheduling for Builders* and has been published in the *ASCE Journal of Construction Engineering and Management*, *The American Institute of Construction Journal*, *Construction Management World*, and other periodicals. Householder has also held seminars on building topics at the NAHB Annual Convention.

Leon Rogers is a professor of Construction Management at Brigham Young University. He is also President of Westek Construction and Consulting, a small residential construction and consulting firm.

One of NAHB's most popular speakers, Rogers has participated in over eighty national seminars on such topics as project management, estimating, scheduling, and financial management. He has been an active member of the NAHB Business Management and Education Committees for over ten years.

Leon Rogers obtained a Ph.D in Urban Planning and Construction Management at Texas A&M University and completed a Masters degree in Construction Management at Colorado State. He has worked with local Home Builders Associations and individual companies to help improve management and has also served as an expert witness in numerous construction law cases on behalf of builders.

The Superintendent's Job

Introduction

The superintendent's job is arguably the most critical responsibility on any job site. In the field, there is little room for error. Money, materials, and labor are on the line and must be carefully controlled. This book has therefore been written specifically for you, the residential construction superintendent responsible for seeing that all field work is performed properly—with no ifs, ands, or buts.

As a condition of this critical responsibility, you must necessarily be concerned with the job as a whole, as well as with the various trades and craftspersons. Yet your specific responsibilities within the company may vary. In a large company, the superintendent usually reports to a project manager, who then reports on up the management line until the owner or chief executive is involved. In smaller construction companies, the superintendent, project manager, and owner are often one and the same. Whether you are also the company owner or several management layers away from the executive office, your number one, primary goal as a superintendent remains the same:

MAXIMIZE PROFITS IN THE LONG TERM

The profit of a construction company is quite easy to determine—simply figure the difference between the sales price and the cost of each house. Obviously, superintendents ordinarily have extremely limited control over the ultimate sales price of the homes they build, with the possible exception of increased sales through quality workmanship and clean, neat job sites. You exercise your greatest influence over company profits in the area of cost. Through conscientious attention to detail and intelligent labor and material decisions, you can influence the final cost of any project significantly. However, while this superintendent influence on project cost is relatively easy to understand, your impact on company profits in the long term may be less clear.

For example, the general philosophy of most businesses is to make the greatest possible profit for the period of time in which the company is in business. If a builder plans to build only one house and then go immediately out of business, a short-sighted, "quick-buck" approach might yield the highest profit. Fortunately, most construction companies plan to stay in business for a relatively long period of time. As a superintendent, your key to success is motivating your workers and subcontractors to bring in every project:

- on time
- at budget
- according to established quality standards

Just about every decision you make as a superintendent should be made in keeping with these three basic responsibilities. Of course, some aspects of your job may be aimed toward the achievement of goals that fail to fall directly under one of these three, such as safety or legal issues. By and large, however, your energies should always be geared toward bringing in a quality job, on time and within budget.

While many of the techniques and examples provided in this manual have specific applications, it is not the purpose of this book to teach you a particular system or point of view. It is hoped that both novice and experienced superintendents will develop both an awareness and an understanding of the primary elements of construction supervision that will result in improved performance and maximum profits for *your* building company.

The Superintendent's Role

A superintendent's responsibilities vary greatly with the size of the company and the leadership strategy of its owners. In a large construction company, your responsibilities as a superintendent might be limited to a single job site, or even to a single segment of the job, such as framing or concrete work.

In the majority of construction companies, however, your role will be much more complicated, involving the entire production phase of construction. Therefore, you must have knowledge of every aspect of construction and be familiar with the work of every trade.

The Superintendent's Authority

The amount of authority you have as a superintendent depends upon several factors, including company size and type, scope of the job, and your level of experience. It is essential that every superintendent fully understand the extent of his or her role and authority within the building organization.

Older, more established building companies often define a superintendent's duties and authority specifically. These builders may wish to maintain control of virtually all aspects of the business, requiring only that their superintendents convey their wishes.

Smaller and/or newly formed companies, on the other hand, may offer you greater freedom. Many smaller builders simply want the job done right and expect the superintendent to take over and supervise the entire construction process. These builders are looking for self-motivated, take-charge supervisors who project this image to others.

The Superintendent As the Company's Agent

A superintendent is a company's agent and field representative, and all negotiations, agreements, and contracts you enter into become legal and binding. Therefore, you have a moral and legal obligation to represent a building company's position responsibly and properly. While you may not agree with all decisions made, it is your duty to put the company first and see that all established goals and objectives are achieved. Superintendents must not allow their personal interests to come between the interests of their companies and other individuals.

To many people, superintendents are their companies. You direct—and often hire and fire—most company employees and usually have more direct contact with persons both inside and outside the organization than anyone else in a building company. In addition, you may often schedule subcontractors, order materials, inspect to ensure quality work, and even deal with customers. Therefore, you can substantially improve a company's image and reputation by being an effective superintendent.

The Superintendent's Duties

As mentioned earlier, a superintendent has many responsibilities in several areas of a construction business. Job descriptions are often used to establish superintendent duties and lines of authority. They should define and document your primary responsibilities and establish a basis for performance evaluation. Job descriptions should also be specific about the relative amount of time and attention that should be devoted to each duty. Examples of items commonly included in a superintendent job description are shown in Figure 1.

The Superintendent As Leader

As a key member of a builder's management team, you must also add leadership to your list of superintendent responsibilities. Leadership is the ability to work with and get things done through others while winning their respect, confidence, loyalty, and cooperation. While many are encumbered by the "born leader" mentality, the fact remains that leadership is an art that can be acquired and developed by anyone with the necessary motivation.

Leadership Basics

To get the best from your subordinates, you should allow them some input and discussion in the decision-making process. Of course, responsibility for any final decision rests with you, the superintendent. However, information, cooperation, and suggestions from those who will actually perform the work can be valuable. With more and more building companies subcontracting much of their work, the superintendent works directly with several different, completely independent businesspersons. The more independent these subcontractors are, the more cooperation and coordination required. When traditional, "bull of the woods" superintendents try to force their will upon today's workers and independent subcontractors, many of

6

Figure 1: A superintendent's duties

I. To build the project according to the quality required.
A. Understand basic techniques and principles of each phase of construction.
   1. Have on-the-job experience.
   2. Attend seminars/training sessions.
   3. Read articles and books on the latest techniques.
B. Read and interpret plans and specifications.
C. Use subcontractors whose work is known.
D. Communicate the required standards to workers.
E. Establish and implement procedures for inspecting worker output.
F. Inspect materials as they are delivered.
G. Report results of inspections to the office in a formal manner.

II. To build the project within the budget.
A. Be familiar with all aspects of the project budget.
B. Use subcontractors who are financially sound.
C. Search for subcontractors who are less expensive and deliver good quality.
D. Suggest alternative methods or materials that are less expensive and meet the required quality standards.
E. Check quantity of all materials against invoices.
F. Implement procedures to minimize theft of materials.
   1. Make materials difficult to steal.
   2. Install materials as soon as possible after delivery.
   3. Arrange for someone to guard isolated or at-risk projects during vulnerable periods.
G. Keep accurate records, and report all expenditures that are not otherwise accounted for in some other manner.

H. Establish and implement procedures for the care and maintenance of all equipment.
I. Follow through on all established procedures for implementing change orders.
J. Follow all established procedures related to material purchases.

III. To build the project on schedule.
A. Understand scheduling methods, including CPM.
B. Be in agreement with—or effect change of—projected completion date.
C. Ensure that subcontractors and suppliers are given sufficient notice.
D. Coordinate material deliveries.
E. Coordinate the work of all subcontractors and hired personnel.
F. Update progress of each project on CPM diagrams (if applicable) on a daily basis.
G. Implement recovery procedures when schedules slip.

IV. Other duties.
A. Establish and enforce safety rules and regulations.
B. Work with buyers.
   1. Coordinate changes according to established procedures.
   2. Keep buyers up-to-date on scheduling projections.
   3. Emphasize quality of materials and workmanship when talking with buyers.

these workers will rebel and refuse to work. Therefore, as an effective leader, you must set an example of proficiency, goodwill, and discipline to get the maximum cooperation from your subordinates.

Most leadership styles can be characterized by the particular emphasis each places on the decision-making process. At one extreme is company-centered leadership, in which the desires and needs of the company come first. At the other extreme is the subordinate-centered leadership style, which puts the needs of employees first. However, the most effective leadership maintains a balance between the needs of the building company and those of the individual worker, often requiring a dynamic, forceful individual to conduct and coordinate activities.

You may want to vary your leadership style with each particular situation. This process will often result in the establishment of leadership precedents—choosing an approach to accomplish the objectives involved in one situation and using that style for all similar situations. Specific leadership styles often found in the construction industry are discussed below.

Dictatorial

In this traditional leadership style, also referred to as autocratic leadership, superintendents keep all power themselves and delegate nothing to subordinates. The superintendent makes all decisions; discussion and suggestions are not permitted. To employ this leadership style successfully, you must become an expert manager of people and be proficient in subordinates' crafts and/or skills. This type of leadership is most appropriate in the following situations:

- in an emergency
- when an extremely tight schedule must be met
- when an employee directly challenges your authority as a superintendent
- when an employee is stubborn or difficult to work with
- when a new employee is being oriented to the job

Bureaucratic

This leadership style relies heavily on established rules, regulations, policies, and procedures to govern the organization. The leader simply enforces the various regulations. This style works best when activities must be performed according to a strict plan, such as when equipment must be installed.

Democratic

The "we" or team approach to leadership allows subordinates to participate in company goal-setting. This style works best when:

- Workers are well-educated, experienced, and motivated.
- Schedules include time for subordinates' participation.
- Problems must be solved.
- Grievances need to be aired and tensions relieved.

Many employees today are motivated and competent enough to work well under democratic leadership.

Orchestration

A leader using orchestration treats employees as members of an orchestra, with the superintendent as the conductor. For this leadership style to be effective, all workers must be highly skilled at their jobs and motivated to work and succeed independently. They must also possess a pride in their work. Orchestration should be restricted to situations in which:

- Skilled, experienced personnel can meet their responsibilities with complete confidence.
- Outside experts, consultants, or similar temporary employees are used.
- A new supervisor lacks experience in the company's day-to-day operations.

Independent workers who are paid according to their output, such as subcontractors and real estate salespersons, tend to prefer this leadership style.

The Superintendent As Manager

A superintendent is part of a management team. Therefore, you should be trained as a manager and act primarily in that capacity. In too many companies, superintendents brought up through the trades are placed in supervisory positions without even the most basic management training. This lack of training can prove detrimental when novice superintendents suddenly find themselves overseeing production and quality control, rather than producing the work themselves. As a manager, your performance is measured by what others do. How well you motivate workers to produce is a key measurement in your success.

People who study management often subdivide it into four basic elements: planning, organizing, directing, and controlling. The effective superintendent must apply these elements in order to reach the three goals of bringing the job in on time, within the budget, and according to the quality standards established. By understanding and applying these basics on your jobs, you can become a better superintendent.

Planning

Someone once summarized management planning in the following way:

"Plan your work, and work your plan."

Planning is the most basic management function, requiring that you simply figure out what must be done. When planning, you develop a program of action to achieve stated goals through the use of people, materials, and financial resources. While superintendents are responsible for planning all the activities that come under their direction, you must also implement the plans of upper management. The saying "Proper planning prevents poor performance" holds especially true in the building industry. Problems arise when no overall objectives are established, when policies and programs conflict, or when procedures are wasteful or poorly thought out.

Planning Made Easy

One of the easiest yet most effective methods of planning involves making a list of all things to be done each day. This method, which is often used by top managers in big business, requires that you start a new list every day, carrying over those tasks not completed from the previous day's list and checking off completed items. Trying to carry around a list of half a dozen tasks in your head takes up valuable storage space in your memory. By putting these items down on paper, you free up your brain to do more productive things.

Organizing

The tasks of planning work and organizing work often overlap. Once you have determined what needs to be done during the planning stage, you must organize the job, determining who is going to perform the work and how completion of the task fits into the overall scheme.

The organization of workers and subcontractors boils down to three questions, which can essentially be combined as one:

"Who does what by when?"

This simple formula is the key to getting things done. The "who" question requires you to allocate personnel and other resources to accomplish the task. It also involves the establishment or use of lines of authority and responsibility for the assigned workers. "What" determines exactly the tasks to be performed. Finally, "when," the phase of organization most often overlooked, must be addressed. The scheduling chapter of this book will explain how to schedule activities on the job site for maximum efficiency.

There are two additional organizational factors you must consider. The first is your own authority as a superintendent to organize workers to perform a certain task. The second is a clearly understood policy controlling hiring and firing, which will allow you to maximize your organizational efforts.

Directing and Coordinating

As you may already be well aware, directing and coordinating take the majority of a superintendent's time. Therefore, these efforts must be targeted directly at the primary goal. If planning is complete and objectives are reasonable, all activities should conform to them, with any deviations corrected through effective control procedures. You should spend most of your time on those areas critical to company success. If progress is being made according to the plan, no action is needed. Routine matters are handled through routine policies and procedures. Only extraordinary items falling beyond preset standards require management attention. Of course, any deviations important to upper management should be reported in a daily or weekly report.

Controlling

Superintendents are directly involved in controlling activities, including control of materials, construction methods, labor, waste prevention, and costs. In addition, you will ordinarily have the authority to decide quantities and cost of labor used, as well as the selection of subcontractors.

Superintendent Control System and Reports. Your entire control system should be economical—detailed enough to highlight deviations, yet not so detailed as to become burdensome or overly expensive. While complex controls can be extremely useful, they often become so complex that they are rarely or never used. Therefore, your reports should be timely, but not time-consuming, always keeping in mind that management needs to keep current on job progress in order to make accurate, sound decisions.

Accounting and Control. You must also keep accounting personnel informed of cost-related activities in order for the accounting system to work effectively. Much of this information can come from the progress report. In some instances, the accounting department has its own forms that require information from the superintendent. You should be careful to safeguard this financial information on a "need-to-know" basis and use it wisely.

The superintendent must carefully review subcontractor payments. Work must be completed satisfactorily prior to authorization of payment. You should have a basic understanding of lien laws as they pertain to a builder's financial liability in order to prevent possible legal problems with subcontractors.

Construction Activities

A large part of your responsibilities as a superintendent will involve the coordination of the basic elements of construction: materials, labor, equipment, subcontractors, customers, financial resources, and time. Each of these elements depends upon the others. A well-organized system in the hands of an effective manager is needed to coordinate these elements and the essential activities related to them: scheduling, staffing, estimating, and evaluation.

Scheduling

Superintendents should select a scheduling system appropriate for each job. You may use critical path method (CPM), a bar chart, a time line, or some other form of scheduling. Since you will ultimately be responsible for employee and subcontractor deadlines, you should be actively involved in determining the overall schedule, establishing contingency plans, and evaluating alternatives. Once established, you will also be charged with enforcing the schedule and seeing that the work progresses smoothly and is done to the builder's satisfaction (see Chapter 5, "Schedule Control").

Staffing

As a superintendent, you have the authority to hire and fire. In addition, you are responsible for training all site personnel and subcontractors regarding acceptable quality standards, operating procedures, construction methods, production efficiency, and company policies and procedures.

Estimating

Estimating may be performed by estimators or by someone else in the company, depending upon the company's size. In most companies, superintendents are not asked to estimate jobs but are expected to build the structure according to the estimate. Because you probably know more about the actual construction process than anyone else involved, you should be an information source for the estimator, providing accurate, reliable information that will lower the chances of estimating errors.

Evaluation

Managers in many businesses frequently say, "Superior managers get superior results." As a member of the management team, you receive part of the credit for building a profitable, growing business. Your performance as a superintendent should therefore be evaluated regularly according to previously established objectives. The self-evaluation form at the end of this chapter (Figure 2) will help you measure your progress and guide you in upgrading your performance.

Figure 2. Self-evaluation form

Rate yourself to find your strengths and weaknesses, then work to improve the latter through reading, formal training, or education; consultation; and conversation with others.

	Frequently	Often	Seldom	Never
Time management				
Do I complete projects on time?	☐	☐	☐	☐
Do I motivate others to do the designated amount of work in the designated time?	☐	☐	☐	☐
Do I control the quality of work performed on my projects?	☐	☐	☐	
Personal				
Am I growing, learning, becoming more of an asset to the company?	☐	☐	☐	☐
Do I set goals for myself?	☐	☐	☐	☐
Do I seek self-improvement through seminars, study, schooling or consultations with others in the field?	☐	☐	☐	☐
Interpersonal performance				
Do I establish performance goals for others?	☐	☐	☐	☐
Do I evaluate the performance of others on the basis of these goals?	☐	☐	☐	☐
Do I receive cooperation from others?	☐	☐	☐	☐
Am I respected?	☐	☐	☐	☐
Training of others				
Do I encourage training and establish the means for it?	☐	☐	☐	☐
Can I motivate others to their maximum potential?	☐	☐	☐	☐
Do I have the courage and fortitude for hiring and firing?	☐	☐	☐	☐
Do I reward superior performance?	☐	☐	☐	☐
With praise?	☐	☐	☐	☐
With consideration?	☐	☐	☐	☐
With monetary means?	☐	☐	☐	☐
With other types of remuneration?	☐	☐	☐	☐
Do I measure my own performance based upon the improvement of others?	☐	☐	☐	☐
Do I listen effectively, both to subordinates and to superiors?	☐	☐	☐	☐
Can I communicate or carry out requests of both subordinates and superiors?	☐	☐	☐	☐
Do I let others carry the responsibility?	☐	☐	☐	☐
Or do I step in and take over for them?	☐	☐	☐	☐

Figure 2. Self-evaluation form (cont.)

	Frequently	Often	Seldom	Never
Can I step in and take over for others when it is absolutely necessary without adversely affecting their morale?	☐	☐	☐	☐
Organization				
Do I have an appearance of organization?	☐	☐	☐	☐
Do I get results by organization through office work?	☐	☐	☐	☐
Do I schedule my own time and the time of others appropriately?	☐	☐	☐	☐
Delegation of duties				
Do I delegate duties appropriately?	☐	☐	☐	☐
Do I assume responsibilities for those duties which I delegate?	☐	☐	☐	☐
Do I follow the lines of authority, both up and down?	☐	☐	☐	☐
Can I work under pressure?	☐	☐	☐	☐
Can I maintain self control?	☐	☐	☐	☐
Can I control the situation rather than permitting the situation to control me?	☐	☐	☐	☐
Management concepts				
Do I set objectives?	☐	☐	☐	☐
Do I establish a plan to achieve the objectives?	☐	☐	☐	☐
Do I set major limitations and controls?	☐	☐	☐	☐
Do I measure the performance of others on the basis of previously established objectives?	☐	☐	☐	☐
Am I aware of the status of all important aspects of the jobs?	☐	☐	☐	☐
Do I have to delay decision making to look up the answers?	☐	☐	☐	☐
Do I keep adequate records on each individual job?	☐	☐	☐	☐
Are the records adequate enough to cover essential elements but not cumbersome or time consuming?	☐	☐	☐	☐
Can I coordinate all the essential elements of construction including the performance of subcontractors, suppliers and others?	☐	☐	☐	☐
Cost control				
Am I cost conscious?	☐	☐	☐	☐
Do I control cost discretely?	☐	☐	☐	☐
Do I foster cost consciousness in others?	☐	☐	☐	☐
Do I control waste?	☐	☐	☐	☐

2

Project Start-Up

Introduction

As the building company's field representative, you are responsible for project management and control. Therefore, you must effectively and conscientiously administer a construction program in a way that meets the primary objective of maximizing profits in the long term while maintaining good business relationships with suppliers, subcontractors, inspectors, and others. As the superintendent, you must bring all available resources to bear upon the timely, cost-effective completion of the project. An effective, conscientious superintendent with the necessary authority and resources can exercise careful control, decrease costs, meet tight schedules, and ensure high-quality work. Without the necessary authority and resources, however, the inevitable result is loss of control, increased costs, prolonged schedules, and poor quality.

Starting Off Right

A project that starts off right has a much better chance of finishing up successfully. On the other hand, a project starting off on the wrong foot may be doomed from the beginning. For example, many a superintendent starts out a job "half-cocked," without adequate planning and control. Consequently, subcontractors fail to show up or arrive to find other subs already working on the job. The superintendent scratches his head and looks over at the hired crew, who are taking long breaks, performing work poorly, and quitting every few weeks, leaving employment gaps that are becoming more and more difficult to fill. This superintendent must spend too much time, money, and energy "putting out fires" that should never have been allowed to spark.

You can ensure that your jobs start off right with

good preliminary planning and scheduling. Planning completed prior to the start of construction will free up time later, when attention needs to be focused on construction progress.

Preconstruction

The superintendent should be actively involved in preconstruction activities. Several key elements in the successful planning of preconstruction activities include the following:

- Determine the key personnel to be used on the project.
- Discuss with key personnel how major administrative requirements can be met, and construction activities carried out.
- Have key personnel review the plans and specifications to determine labor requirements.

Site Considerations

As the company's field representative, you are normally responsible for evaluating most site considerations relating to overall job progress and profitability. For example, you may be called upon to evaluate such conditions as high water tables in areas where basements are specified, or areas where the slope of the lot or soil conditions do not permit building a home according to the plan. The superintendent is usually turned to first, as the best resource for resolving site problems.

Project and Site Logistics

In addition to being responsible for—and taking direct charge of—site layout, you should also be concerned with such site logistics as access, water, electrical, and others. A site visit report developed by the Associated General Contractors gives super-

13

intendents a checklist to follow when visiting a job site for the first time (Figure 3).

Arrange for Utilities. Utilities must be made readily available so that subcontractors and other workers do not have to waste time stringing extension cords great distances in order to obtain power or running long hoses to obtain water.

Organize the Physical Layout. Laying out the site on most larger jobs involves the efficient placement of the storage area, office, and areas for fabrication, if required. The objective of an effective physical layout is to ensure that work can be performed efficiently. Every physical site has its own special set of conditions that make this layout unique. For example, your requirements for a cramped downtown site will be much different from those for a rural location.

Set up a field office and storage shed. Your field office may be nothing more than a portable shed or designated area containing a small desk or plan table and a telephone. On scattered sites, a pick-up truck and cellular phone may be the only "office" available. On a large project, a field office can be a particularly effective time-saver, giving the superin-tendent a central location from which to control the project. A storage area should be located where it will not interfere with other activities, yet still be as close as possible to the areas where the stored materials will be used.

Prepare for Surface Water Control. Once started, grading should be completed as quickly as possible to minimize continuing disturbance of the soil. Open trenches should be covered as soon as possible. Straw bales or silt fences should be ready for use in controlling and filtering runoff; rock or gravel may also be needed for filtering. Consider using temporary collecting ponds in the event of unforeseen, severe wet weather.

Schedules

The construction schedule will dictate the sequence of construction: which activities must follow one another? For example, if the interior trim is to be stained, it would be best to stain this trim and paint the interior walls before the trim is installed. However, if the trim is to be painted, then it would be better to install the trim first.

Deliveries need to be scheduled so that materials

Figure 3. Site visit report*

Site Visit by _____ Date _____

_____

_____

Name of development_____

Owner _____

Location of development_____

Date of Visit_____

Distance to closest towns or cities _____

Highways

Type and surface condition _____

Capacities of bridges or load restrictions _____

Site access and security

What is the traffic flow? _____

What are the restrictions on size of vehicle that can get onto the site? _____

_____

---

* Adapted with permission from *Project Management Supervisory Training Program*, Unit 8, Copyright 1979 by Associated General Contractors of America.

Figure 3. Site visit report (cont.)

How many entrances does the site have or need? _____

What are the security requirements? _____

On-site access roads

What material (existing dirt, gravel, fill, etc.) should be used? _____
_____

Is local road-surfacing material available? _____

Will drainage be a problem? _____

What kind of maintenance will be required? _____
_____

Will the roads be interrupted or restricted by underground or overhead utilities? _____
_____

Will temporary roads or driveways be needed? _____ Where? _____

What types of signs and how many will be required to efficiently direct people to the jobsite? _____
_____

Describe any potential bottlenecks _____

Electrical power

Name of supplier _____

Address _____

Closest installation and capacity description _____

Cost of extension or installation on job _____

Person to contact for installation _____ Phone (___) _____

Telephone

Person to contact for installation _____ Phone (___) _____

Distance to and location of nearest pay phone? _____

Water

Determine availability of potable water _____

Other sources of water _____

Weather

Describe typical weather, possible extreme weather conditions, and length of working season. _____
_____

Unions

Hiring hall locations _____

Health, welfare, pension, vacation funds _____

Travel pay and dispatch points _____

Secure copies of current contracts with pay schedules _____

Supply of common and skilled labor in area _____

Predominant industry (agriculture, timber, manufacturing, etc.) _____

Figure 3. Site visit report (cont.)

Local subcontractors or suppliers

Adequacy of plant, shop, warehouse, method of delivery, reputation _____
_____

Construction material suppliers

Lumber _____

Aggregate _____

Rock and fill materials _____

Clearing _____

Painting _____

Mechanical _____

Electrical _____

Ready mix plants _____

Rental equipment _____

Framing _____

Landscaping _____

Other _____

Other _____

Other _____

☐ Obtain copy of telephone directory

Visit owner's office (if applicable)

List names, titles, and telephone numbers of persons contacted

Name _____

Title _____ Phone (___) _____

Name _____

Title _____ Phone (___) _____

Name _____

Title _____ Phone (___) _____

Discuss general job requirement _____
_____
_____

Clarify questioned items in specifications _____
_____
_____

Pollution regulations _____

Safety requirements _____

Construction easements _____

Landmarks _____

   Take conducted tour of proposed worksite _____

   Examine all cores and logs of test holes available _____

Figure 3. Site visit report (cont.)

Describe site _____

_____

Identify any unusual surface or subsurface conditions such as unusually rocky conditions. _____

_____

General discussion of site considerations _____

_____

_____

_____

Take photographs of all planted areas and general construction areas. _____

Office location and layout (if applicable)

Can office or work area be located on the property? _____ If not, where should it be located? _____

_____

Do subs need office area? _____

Will later operations cause it to be relocated? _____

Can it be located to allow key personnel to view the bulk of the project from the office? _____

_____

Is parking space adequate? _____

Is a craft or storage shed provided? _____

Estimate work required to prepare site _____

_____

_____

Major storage areas

Will storage area have to be fenced? _____

How far will storage be from the work? _____

Will it allow easy access from the field? _____

Will mechanical loading and moving of material be possible inside the storage area? _____

What material will be first in? _____

What material will be first out? _____

Will an enclosed warehouse be required? _____

Will it have to be heated? _____

What security precautions need to be taken? _____

Onsite storage

Will onsite storage allow for uninterrupted movement of construction traffic? _____

_____

Have future activities such as underground utilities, site cuts, and fills been considered? _____

_____

Is access to onsite storage good? _____

are available when needed, but not so early that they take up valuable storage space for an excessively long time—or disappear before they are used. Workers should not have to move materials to accommodate or avoid subcontractors. Through planning and careful scheduling, such conflicts can be avoided.

Regulations

Superintendents should always keep informed of local ordinances and regulations pertaining to their jobs and make certain to obtain all necessary permits. Discussing how best to comply with regulations, policies, and procedures with local building code officials will help you avoid problems at inspection time. Failure to comply with any regulation can mean considerable delays and, in some cases, fines for the builder. Inspectors may also require that perfectly good work be torn out if the necessary requirements are not met.

Defining Subcontractor Responsibilities

On a given project, one of your first responsibilities is often taking bids on work to be subcontracted and awarding the subcontracts.

Pre-Bid Procedures. Prior to receiving subcontractor bids, you must determine how much each area of work should cost to assist in bid evaluation. When requesting bids, you should control subcontractor overlap and prevent gaps from occurring by clarifying and defining the exact scope of each subcontract or agreement. You might also arrange to have work not adequately described in the contract documents included as part of a specific subcontractor's agreement. For example, does the footing subcontractor lay out the foundation on the footings, or is that job someone else's responsibility? Does the framer install felt paper on the roof, or is that job performed by the roofing subcontractor? You will also want to determine who is responsible for clean-up of subcontractor operations and removal of trash from the job site. Responsibilities such as these must be clarified in order for construction to flow smoothly.

Bid Review and Selection. With this information in hand, you can proceed with bid review and the issuing of subcontracts and major purchase orders. If authorized, you should participate in evaluating all bids and awarding the contracts to the various low bidders. In some companies, this part of the process may be reserved exclusively for the builder. However, if you are going to be responsible for subcontractor coordination, you should also lend a hand to ensure that each subcontractor understands the line of authority and the position of responsibility.

Construction Documents. To meet responsibilities, every superintendent must be familiar with the construction documents for each job, including the plans, specifications, and each subcontract agreement. You should have a basic understanding of contract law, including an understanding of the type of notice required to protect the company if the subcontractor defaults, and the liabilities a construction company incurs when a superintendent issues instructions that may be contrary to regulations, laws, or safety rules. In addition, you will want to be familiar with all the requirements of an enforceable contract, including the following:

- work
- price
- time
- delivery
- payment provisions
- liens
- liquidated damages
- bidding mistakes
- termination
- change orders
- contract interpretation
- changed conditions
- submittals
- owner responsibilities

Other Responsibilities

As the field superintendent, you will serve as a resource for the subcontractor, answering questions, clarifying unclear areas, and solving problems. Another of your responsibilities will be to ensure that all necessary equipment is safe, adequately maintained, and available to those who will be using it. Necessary accessories should be included, such as oil, saw blades, and power cords.

Preconstruction Meetings

One of the tools used almost universally in commercial construction and being adopted more frequently in residential construction is the preconstruction coordination meeting. The basis of this meeting can be a company procedures and policies manual, which is often distributed to each participant in a large, complex project.

The objective of the preconstruction meeting is to establish the responsibilities and expectations of each participant. Lines of communication must be established among all participants, including both the regular channels of authority and the communication procedures listed below:

- schedules
- acceptance of work
- inspections
- change orders
- safety
- payment
- disputes

The preconstruction meeting also informs all participants of what is expected of them during the course of construction. In addition, the overall format of the construction process is explained. The meeting establishes the ground rules for the policies and procedures that will be enforced during construction, with cooperation and commitment solicited from participants. The developer or builder, superintendent, design professional, subcontractors, and major suppliers should attend, providing them with an opportunity to coordinate efforts and understand more fully how each participant contributes to overall project progress. On smaller jobs, a formal meeting as described here may be deemed unnecessary. If such a meeting is not held, the superintendent should meet with all project participants individually and cover the same information discussed in the following sections.

Planning the Meeting. Proper planning can make meeting time more productive for everyone. You should prepare an itemized agenda for distribution to participants so that they can reserve questions or comments until the appropriate time. The meeting facility should be conveniently located, comfortable, and conducive to a successful meeting.

Conducting the Meeting. When conducting a preconstruction meeting, you should:

- Be sure that the person assigned to take minutes is present.
- Begin on time and maintain control of the meeting.
- Establish ground rules.
- Define items to be discussed.
- Stick to the agenda.
- Obtain scheduling commitments from subcontractors.
- Solve problems.

- Summarize decisions made.
- Solicit questions and feedback from all participants.
- Set time aside for new business.

During the meeting, you will also want to examine and discuss the construction schedule and point out critical dates for delivery of materials and completion of various phases of the project. Subcontractors should also receive tentative dates for start-up of their work, discussing the schedule and resolving any conflicts that may exist. In addition, you should solicit a commitment from each subcontractor and supplier to comply with the schedule *as agreed upon*. Penalties for noncompliance should then be clearly defined and established. Each individual's responsibility with regard to customer callbacks and warranties must also be outlined, and a procedure for problem-solving established. Finally, minutes of the meeting should be distributed to all participants.

Identifying Problems. As problems come up during the course of the preconstruction meeting, keep an open mind to the alternatives and solutions suggested. Discussing problems without proposing or accepting viable solutions wastes time (unless further information is required). Methods of carrying out solutions, measuring results, and reporting back to the group must be established.

Construction

Reports and Documents

Superintendents sometimes attempt to control a project with little more than a vague recollection of past performance on other projects. "Seat of the pants" management is a major cause of poor control on a construction project, and poor reporting practices are usually a large contributor. On the other hand, you may often find yourself deluged with more information than you can possibly use in controlling the project. What is needed is a balance between these two extremes that allows you to obtain the exact level of detail and amount of information required.

Effective documents and reports can provide just such a balance. Reports documenting what actually occurred on a project can do the following:

- Inform company management of project status at any given time.
- Establish projections of future activities.
- Assist in job control.

Adequate documentation is also necessary in requesting change orders. Without proper documentation, pricing change orders and requesting payment for items beyond the scope of the contract are impossible.

Accuracy. In order for construction documents and reports to have any legal credibility, they must be accurate. Superintendents should be careful to note any specific details immediately to ensure the accuracy of all documented information.

Completeness. The superintendent must make certain that reports contain all information needed to manage and control the job properly. While remembering everything that happened on a construction job is impossible, you should document in writing any important occurrences at the time they occur. Some superintendents carry a pad of paper or notebook and are continually jotting down items they need to remember. Others carry a small tape recorder to eliminate confusion and the time involved in writing, having the information transcribed later.

Objectivity. Reports must be objective to be acceptable. Facts should be presented without interjecting opinions.

Uniformity. Reports should be provided on a standardized form or in a standardized format, facilitating comparisons with previous reports. Samples of several useful construction reports are found in Chapter 3, "Quality Control and Inspections."

Believability. By documenting all necessary items in a timely and unbiased manner, you establish credibility as a superintendent. Most people can readily discern an altered or biased report. Handwritten reports are generally more acceptable in legal proceedings when they are documented and bound in such a way that pages cannot be moved or added. Original notes should never be modified; if something is forgotten and remembered later, add this information to another report at a later date. Do not alter an earlier report to put the information in its "proper" place.

Timeliness. Timely reports are one of the key elements in improving communications and eliminating misunderstandings. To effectively manage and make informed decisions, reports must be completed regularly in order to be as up-to-date as possible.

Types of Reports

Daily Reports. The daily report or activities log on the job site (see Figures 4 and 5) is generally a

Figure 4. Items to be included in a daily report

(Items to be included in the daily report need not be limited to this list.)

Job Conditions
- A complete description of the weather for the day including both high and low temperatures, and in as much detail as necessary to document delays caused by weather
- Any problems that arise related to utilities, access to the site, drainage, snow removal, and anything related to site conditions and facilities
- All visitors to the job site who are not directly involved in the construction process such as inspectors, owners, architects, building officials, safety inspectors, government officials

Activities
- Information received from the owner or design professional including the selection of items, colors, change orders, and accessories
- Work started, completed, or in progress
- Labor problems including disputes or disagreements
- All accidents, including who was involved, witnesses, the circumstances surrounding the accident, the results, and any implications for safety authorities
- Major material deliveries and or delays
- Purchase orders issued from the field or material purchased

Subcontractors
- Subcontractors who start or complete work and work in progress
- The work force of each subcontractor on the job and major changes in the job
- Itemize questions to and from subcontractors
- Record instructions to subcontractors and follow up with memorandums
- Describe any disagreements with subcontractors or suppliers on the job site

Communications from the owner, builder, architect, inspector
- All change orders requested and the status of each change
- Directives given by owners, inspectors, and others
- Any unusual circumstances or problems encountered as a result of these directives

Schedule
- Work completed
- Work in progress
- Work to be started in the immediate future
- Problems that relate to the schedule

Equipment
- All equipment present on the job site that day
- Equipment needs
- Rentals and returns
- Breakdown and repairs
- Other equipment problems

Contacts
- All phone conversations or personal contacts, the circumstances of each conversation, and the results

Figure 5. Daily report

Project _____

Weather: ☐ Fair ☐ Overcast ☐ Rain ☐ Snow

Job number _____
Temperature: ☐ 0-50 ☐ 50-80 ☐ 80 up

Superintendent _____
Wind: ☐ Still ☐ Moderate ☐ High

Work force/subcontractors

_____ Foreman	_____ Plumbers	_____ Bricklayers	_____ Cement finishers
_____ Foundation	_____ Electricians	_____ Roofers	_____ Floor covering installers
_____ Framers	_____ Heat & A/C	_____ Tile installers	_____ (other)
_____ Carpenters	_____ Insulators	_____ Painters	_____ (other)
_____ Laborers	_____ Drywallers	_____ Cabinet	_____ (other)

Equipment on job _____
_____

Remarks: _____
_____
_____

Visitors

Time	Name	Representing	Remarks
_____	_____	_____	_____
_____	_____	_____	_____
_____	_____	_____	_____
_____	_____	_____	_____

Equipment needs, rentals, problems _____
_____
_____

Work completed (describe) _____
_____
_____

Work in progress (describe) _____
_____
_____

Remarks, phone conversations, contacts, problems: _____
Work in progress (describe status) _____
_____
_____

(Signature)

hand-written account, preferably in a bound book. Daily reports have greater legal credibility than almost any account of job activity. Therefore, you must maintain these reports accurately, including *all* items of importance and particularly any item that might become the subject of a disagreement.

Daily reports have four basic purposes:

- To provide a record of activities.
- To make immediate note of instructions given verbally to ensure that action is taken and that the action is justified.
- To back up future change order requests and additional charges.
- For possible use in any dispute settlements, arbitration, or lawsuits.

Progress Reports. These reports summarize the status of each phase of the project (see Figure 6). They perform the following functions for project managers and builders:

- Communicate project status to company management and others.
- Summarize information contained in daily logs.
- Summarize instructions and decisions made regarding subcontractors and suppliers.

- Summarize progress compared with the schedule.
- Allow coordination between the office and project superintendent by assembling the information in an organized fashion.

The progress report and the daily report should complement each other, with the progress report summarizing the daily report and communicating this necessary information to those involved in the project. Progress reports may be sent to subcontractors, suppliers, and the owner and design professional.

Safety

Safety and health are as much a part of project planning and control as any other aspect of construction. As the superintendent, you are primarily responsible for ensuring that construction workers have a safe and healthy place in which to work, a responsibility mandated by law and required by government regulations. The Occupational Safety and Health Act, federal legislation dealing with safety and health in the construction industry, was an effort on the part of Congress to establish uniform standards throughout all industries to ensure and mandate adequate safety on the job.

Figure 6. Items to be included in a progress report

Communication to the owner
- Decisions and action required from the owner
- Delays experienced and their causes
- Verbal instructions and information received from the owner
- Change order requests and their status

Information for subcontractors and suppliers
- The status of each contract or major purchase order
- Summarize instructions and changes occurring during the week
- Items requiring coordination in current work
- Give notice of future performance requirements or schedule changes

Progress versus schedule
- Summarize the status of the schedule as nearly as possible, compare the current with the scheduled status of the project, and outline any variances
- Describe the impact on the project of delays by the owner

Problems
- Summarize problems, their apparent causes, and proposed solutions

Safety on the job must begin with the individuals working on the site. Workers should begin each project with the belief that safety on the job is a personal concern as well as the concern of every other worker on the project. Each worker should therefore be aware of safety hazards and correct them regardless of the existence of rules and regulations to eliminate them. However, because workers often fail in this most basic form of safety management, builders and contractors must establish their own safety rules and programs.

The Dangers of the Construction Site. The construction industry has traditionally been a difficult industry in which to work. At times, work is performed under adverse weather conditions and involves the use of hazardous materials, tools, and equipment. Others hazards include noise, dust, explosions, as well as the potential for falling or being struck by falling material and equipment. Resulting injuries can prove catastrophic in terms of loss of life and personal injury.

Liability Problems. The recent tendency of the courts toward larger and larger settlements on behalf of parties injured as a result of inadequate protection on the job is alarming. Superintendents and their building companies must establish an atmosphere of safety and become conscious of possible violations or unsafe conditions on the job.

Organizational Image. Any building company's public image can be seriously damaged or even destroyed by a single accident resulting from careless and/or unsafe conditions on a job site. It can prove almost impossible for a builder to live down the poor reputation resulting from a needless fatality due to an unsafe condition. In addition, the adverse publicity can be devastating. In one case, a five-year-old boy drowned in a hole dug for a septic tank on one construction site. The resulting lawsuit and negative publicity were factors in the parent organization's later declaration of bankruptcy. This result is not uncommon, and the personal grief suffered by persons involved in a fatal accident never truly ceases.

Hazardous Communication Guidelines. While on the job, every person has a right to expect to be protected from obvious hazards and illness. However, building companies and their superintendents are also now faced with the task of informing their workers regarding certain job-related hazards that may not be quite so obvious. The Occupational Safety and Health Administration (OSHA) currently has full and immediate authority to conduct HazCom inspections of all construction companies and job sites. Citations and possible fines of up to $10,000 per violation have been issued for non-compliance.

All building companies and contractors, no matter how large or small, are required to comply with the HazCom Standard. Employers must inform and train their employees about all hazardous substances they are working with, as well as those materials they might come into contact with from other trades. There are four main elements of HazCom compliance:

- Preparing a written Hazard Communication Program for your company
- Labeling products and containers
- Providing Material Safety Data Sheets
- Training employees

The National Association of Home Builders, Associated Builders and Contractors, and the American Subcontractors Association have developed a comprehensive, step-by-step compliance kit that has been praised by OSHA. This Hazardous Communication Kit is available from NAHB's Business Management Department.

3

Quality Control and Inspections

Introduction

Of the superintendent's three primary responsibilities, quality control will have the greatest impact on overall long-term success. Quality control on the construction site is based on three basic responsibilities:

- Recognizing the performance standards required for both materials and workmanship.
- Judging whether or not completed work meets the established standards.
- Establishing procedures to ensure that these standards are met.

When determining the level of quality required, you are obligated to follow the dictates of those to whom you report. As a matter of policy, upper management will ordinarily establish standards mutually acceptable both to the company and to the homeowner. It then becomes your responsibility to determine whether or not the work meets these standards.

The best superintendents learn to judge work quality through years of valuable experience. However, less-experienced superintendents can upgrade their skills in various ways:

- Talking with experienced superintendents and asking questions.
- Reading books and articles on the subject.
- Using educational audiotapes and videotapes.
- Talking with municipal inspectors.

Responsibility for Quality Control

You should keep in mind that quality control is not the superintendent's exclusive domain, but requires the participation of everyone involved in the construction process: architect, owner, contractor, superintendent, subcontractors, suppliers, and laborers. All members of the building team have a responsibility to ensure that their work meets the mutually accepted standards and that the materials used are of a quality equal to—or better than—the materials specified.

Creating an Atmosphere of High Quality

The best insurance of a high quality job is to maintain a high level of quality control throughout the job. If all work is inspected and approved as the project progresses, fewer problems will develop at inspection time. This emphasis on quality control should begin at the top with upper management and trickle down through the entire company structure. Without this active support, mottos, slogans, and signs are simply wasted effort.

Attitudes also have a direct impact on the quality of construction work. Since every worker possesses an innate desire to do high quality work, you should make every effort to cultivate this attitude and motivate the worker. A company that emphasizes high quality inspires excellent workmanship.

Performance Standards

Performance standards are the basis of any quality control system and should be in writing. These standards communicate to those involved what is to be built, the criteria to be used in judging quality, and the specifications required. Management should devote the time necessary to make certain that all standards are precise, understandable, and based on measurable criteria. Once standards are set, they must be communicated to those responsible for carrying them out. You might find it beneficial to provide employees and subcontractors with a copy of the standards that apply to them.

One company has implemented a program called PRIDE: Personal Responsibility in Daily Excellence. PRIDE is aimed at motivating individual workers to peak performance. It lets employees know how important they are and helps them develop new confidence and self-esteem. By taking responsibility for their own work, employees satisfy their own needs for recognition and praise. In addition, employees responsible for improved quality are given sizable monetary rewards.

Training

Training a company's own workers is generally recognized as a good idea. However, subcontractors and material suppliers can also be trained, leading to greater quality control. This type of training can usually be accomplished through in-house sessions and informal discussions, or through formal seminars sponsored by the National Association of Home Builders and other organizations. Informal inspections and critique sessions conducted by experienced quality control inspectors can also serve as an excellent teaching aid.

Enforcing Standards

All construction team members have the ultimate responsibility of ensuring that their work is equal to or better than the quality specified. However, the superintendent is in the best position to enforce the standards. Performance should be judged on the basis of compliance with the standards, with the individual or firm responsible for the resulting work—and any necessary corrective action.

Inspections

Internal Inspections

Internal inspections must be timely if they are to be of any value. As the superintendent responsible for quality control, you should actively inspect each project daily, even if projects are on widely scattered lots. These checks should verify whether work is progressing as scheduled. They also allow the superintendent to inspect work completed since the last visit.

Building companies without formal quality control systems often rely heavily on public inspectors to detect faults, provide punch lists, or identify corrections. Following this practice is asking for trouble. Each company should conduct its own inspections if it wants to reduce the risk of shoddy work and expensive rework.

Inspection Checklists

When conducting their own inspections, many superintendents use inspection checklists (Figures 7-13) tailored to their particular organization. These checklists serve as a memory jogger, forcing the inspector to look for crucial items. Inspection checklists should include information on any items that:

- have been problems in the past,
- are difficult to repair or replace if they are covered up, and
- are particularly important to quality in the eyes of the customer.

Your company should carefully adapt all quality control checklists to include specific standards that are both measurable and attainable. For example, your company might choose to adapt items in Figure 7, Footing Inspection, as follows:

Footings
(Check all dimensions)

_____ Check for square (1/4" in 10')

_____ Check for depth ($+/- 1$")

_____ Check rebar size, spacing, and number ($+/- 1/2$")

Preinspections

Inspections required by local building codes, FHA/VA, and lending institutions are usually intended only to ensure compliance with standards of safety and structural integrity, rather than to deal specifically with quality control. Nonetheless, you should conduct preinspection checks in order to detect and correct any problems before the inspector arrives. This worthwhile practice can serve several purposes:

- Prevents rejection by the inspector.
- Eliminates the cost of reinspection fees.
- Maintains your company's reputation as a high quality builder.

Gaining Cooperation

During outside inspections, you may find it best to develop a cooperative attitude, extending courtesy toward inspectors whenever possible. Inspectors tend to be more cooperative under such circumstances. To develop this atmosphere of cooperation, you should follow these guidelines:

- Schedule inspections in accordance with the procedures of the inspection department, and as far in advance as possible.
- Make certain that a job is ready before calling for an inspection.
- If a job is not ready when an inspection is scheduled, notify the inspector.
- Be available to the inspector during the inspection whenever possible.
- Cooperate with the inspectors in correcting work that is below standard.
- If the inspector requires something above and beyond the code requirement, find out why. If the reasoning is sound, comply with the request. If compliance seems unreasonable, try negotiating first. Refusing to comply may create hard feelings and can lead to considerable delays while both parties attempt to prove their points. Cooperation is always better than alienation.

Inspection Points

The following inspection points are critical:

- Prior to the placing of concrete footings and foundations.
- Prior to the placing of concrete floors.
- After rough framing.
- Upon completion of rough mechanical work.
- After rough electrical and plumbing.
- When drywall is up (prior to painting).
- Upon completion.

Each of these inspections should be considered mandatory, and each is required by most building inspection departments.

Logging Inspections

All required inspections should be noted on the construction schedule and recorded in the daily log book. The daily log should contain records on both in-house and outside inspections, including the following:

- date and time of the inspection
- name of the inspector
- nature of the inspection
- results of the inspection
- notes on any special circumstances
- inspector's signature

Final Inspection

The final inspection before the customer walk-through and orientation is one of the most important. Your immediate supervisor should conduct this inspection and be very critical of even small discrepancies. This inspection serves as a check-and-balance procedure for the superintendent, whose familiarity with the job day after day may cause him or her to miss small flaws. Being super-critical at this point will cut down on customer complaints and enhance the builder's reputation for quality.

Customer Walk-Through and Orientation

If the proper inspections have already taken place, the customer walk-through and orientation can be a positive, rewarding experience, rather than something to be dreaded by everyone involved. Some builders even invite subcontractors to be present in order to demonstrate the operation and maintenance of their products; subcontractors installing complex systems, such as lawn sprinklers or security systems, are particularly well suited to this approach. They can also explain any warranties involved and discuss how customer service requests will be handled. Their presence helps to make customers aware of their own responsibilities for maintenance and establishes a means of satisfaction for many customer complaints. Instead of simply having the customer look for flaws or imperfections, the positive aspects of the home are accentuated. For further information on the customer walk-through and orientation, see Chapter 7, "Working with the Buyer."

Figure 7. Footing inspection

Job address _____

_____

Lot no. _____
Subdivision _____

Date _____

Initial

Location of property lines

_____ Determine how the property lines were located.
_____ Were property survey stakes in place? ☐ Yes ☐ No
_____ Were property survey stakes clearly identified? ☐ Yes ☐ No

Set backs

_____ Was plot plan available? ☐ Yes ☐ No
_____ Was owner present during layout? ☐ Yes ☐ No
_____ Correct front yard set back _____ Which side? _____
_____ Rear yard set back _____

Ground water

_____ Check for presence of ground water or soft spots

Footings
(Check all dimensions)

_____ Check for square
_____ Check for proper blockouts
_____ Check offsets and jogs: ☐ Location ☐ Size _____
_____ Check for elevation
_____ Check for depth and width
_____ Check to make sure forms are level
_____ Check rebar size, spacing, and number
_____ Check bracing and backfill
_____ Check quantity of concrete ordered, bag mix, and slump

_____
(Signature)

Figure 8. Foundation inspection

Job address _____

_____

Lot no. _____

Subdivision _____

Date _____

Initial **Location**

_____ Check proper setbacks and alignment
_____ How were they established? _____
_____ Thickness of foundation _____

Foundation

_____ Check all dimensions: length _____ width _____ height _____
_____ Offsets: ☐ Location ☐ Size
_____ Fireplace Jogs: ☐ Location ☐ Size
_____ Windows: ☐ Location ☐ Size ☐ Bracing
_____ Bulkheads: ☐ Location
_____ Doors: ☐ Location ☐ Size ☐ Bracing
_____ Blockouts: ☐ Location ☐ Size ☐ Bracing
_____ Beam Pockets: ☐ Size ☐ Location
_____ Walk outs _____ Air entrained concrete only
_____ Adequate ties
_____ Adequate bracing
_____ Plumb—check several places
_____ Square—check all places
_____ Straight
_____ Level
_____ Corbels: ☐ Location ☐ Size

Reinforcing steel

_____ Size _____
_____ Quantity _____
_____ According to code ☐ Local jurisdiction ☐ FHA/VA ☐ Other _____
_____ Location (Explain) _____

_____
(Signature)

Figure 9. Inspection prior to backfill

Job address _____

_____

Lot no. _____

Subdivision _____

Date _____

Initial

_____ Foundation honeycomb, if any, patched and sealed watertight

_____ Tie broken off and all tie holes filled with black plastic cement

_____ Seam between foundation and footing sealed watertight

_____ Foundation waterproofing complete according to quality standards

_____ Footing drains installed properly according to plans where appropriate

_____ All debris and garbage removed from trenches

_____ Check floor drains:
  ☐ Location   ☐ Elevation

_____
(Signature)

Figure 10. Framing inspection

Job address _____

_____

Lot no. _____
Subdivision _____

Date _____

Initial	Floor framing
_____	Sill scaler insulation installed
_____	Foundation bolts secured properly with washers
_____	At least 2 bolts per plate, not more than 16 inches from each end or nailed with power actuated nails
_____	Header joist straight
_____	Header joist toenailed properly with 10d nails
_____	Joists nailed to header with 3-16d nails
_____	Joist hangers installed and nailed where necessary
_____	Plywood glued properly
_____	Plywood nailed 8 inches on center on edges, 12 inches on center at intermediate supports
_____	1/16'' uniform space around each sheet of plywood
_____	Plywood grade stamp correct
_____	Plywood subfloor should overhang stairwell opening to match treads
_____	If bridging used—installed properly
_____	One inch air space around masonry fireplace
_____	Check grade, species, and span of floor joists
_____	Check stair risers to see if all are equal between 7 and 1 inches
_____	Check treads for level
_____	Check stair jacks for cracks

Initial	Wall framing
_____	All walls erected according to plan
_____	Check critical dimensions
_____	All walls square
_____	All walls plumb
_____	Door openings: ☐ Plumb ☐ Square
_____	Swinging doors over carpeted areas 82 inches high, 2 inches wider than door
_____	Bypass doors with jambs and casing 84 inches high—same as width of both doors
_____	Bifold doors with carpet and jambs and casing 82 inches high, 2 inches wider than doors
_____	Bifold doors over linoleum and jambs and casings 81 inches high, 2 inches wider than doors
_____	Bifold doors with sheetrock jambs and linoleum 80½ inches high, 1¼ inches wider than doors
_____	Bifold doors with sheetrock jambs and carpet 81½ inches high, 1½ inches wider than doors
_____	Exterior doors over carpet 83 inches high, 2 inches wider than door
_____	Exterior doors over linoleum 82 inches high, 2 inches wider than door
_____	Pocket doors framed substantially
_____	Windows framed ½ inch wider than window, 1½ inches higher than window
_____	Sliding glass door framed 81 inches high, ½ inch wider

Figure 10. Framing inspection (cont.)

Initial	Wall framing (cont.)

_____ Attic access framed in 22½ × 30

_____ All warped studs removed or
straightened

_____ All backing or drywall clips 24 inches on
center installed

_____ Splices in plates occur over studs

_____ Trimmer stud and header joints tight

_____ All walls, studs, headers, plates nailed
securingly per code

_____ Backing for curtain rods, rings installed

_____ Backing for towel rods, rings installed

_____ Dimensions for cabinet drops checked
and rechecked

_____ Fire blocking installed at cabinet drops

_____ Garage door jambs and brick mold
installed

_____ Bath tub opening 60¼''

_____ Sheathing installed with tight joints and
nailed properly

Initial	Roof Framing

_____ Trusses erected according to plan

_____ Trusses toenailed with 10d nails

_____ Framing anchors installed according to
code

_____ Catwalk installed

_____ Wind brace installed at gable ends

_____ Attic vents installed properly

_____ All gable and firewall trusses have
studding installed 24 inches on center
to relieve sheathing or sheetrock

_____ False fascia and barge rafters installed
straight and secure

_____ Outriggers installed at peak and every
space in soffit if plywood soffit used
on gable ends

_____ Roof sheathing nailed 8 inches on center
on edges and 12 inches on center at
supports

_____ Insulation baffels installed where
required

_____ All debris, trash, cleaned up

_____ All good lumber stacked properly in
shade

_____

(Signature)

Figure 11. Insulation inspection

Job address _____
_____

Lot no. _____
Subdivision _____

Date _____

Initial

_____ Proper insulation with proper R-Value according to plans and specifications installed

_____ Insulation fits snug top and bottom

_____ Insulation placed behind wiring not stuffed in front of or behind box

_____ Gaps around windows insulated or caulked

_____ Gaps around exterior doors insulated or caulked

_____ All pipes and outlet boxes penetrating outside walls caulked or insulated

_____ Header joist insulated properly

Initial

_____ Sill sealer insulation installed

_____ Vapor barrier installed properly:
  ☐ No holes   ☐ Splices overlap
  ☐ Proper thickness

_____ Corners and small holes insulated properly

_____ Plywood box headers insulated

_____ Hot water pipes in uninsulated area wrapped with insulation

_____ Heat ducts in uninsulated area wrapped with insulation

_____ Joists of heat ducts in uninsulated space sealed with duct tape

_____
(Signature)

Figure 12. Finish inspection before paint

Job address _____

_____

Lot no. _____

Subdivision _____

Date _____

Initial **Drywall**

_____ All appropriate drywall installed
_____ Check walls for smooth finish
        everywhere
_____ Check corners for smooth finish
        everywhere
_____ Check for loose nails or pops
_____ Check around windows for proper fit
        finish
_____ Check around outlet boxes for good fit

Doors

_____ All doors installed according to plan
_____ Corners glued on casing and proper fit
_____ Nails adequate and set
_____ Doors swing properly
_____ Doors plumb
_____ Proper clearance to allow for tempera-
        ture and humidity changes
_____ Casing nailed properly—no splits
_____ Pocket doors trimmed properly
_____ Bipass doors trimmed properly
_____ Bifold doors trimmed properly—
        including knobs

Initial **Base**

_____ All base installed
_____ Nails into solid backing and set
_____ Corners coped properly
_____ Base around cabinets tacked in place for
        paint

Shelving

_____ Shelving to plans and specifications
_____ All shelving cut to proper length
_____ Adequate shelf supports attached to
        solid backing
_____ Shelving nailed and glued properly
_____ Check squeaks in floors
_____ Attic access installed properly

_____

(Signature)

34

Figure 13. Final inspection

Job address _____

_____

Lot no. _____

Subdivision _____

Date _____

Initial	Foundation
_____	Ties inside and out broken off
_____	Cracks honeycomb repaired
_____	Plastic bonded securely—no cracks

Site work

_____ 2 percent grade away from house

_____ Final grade smooth and backfill settled
properly

_____ Sidewalks and patio installed according
to plan

_____ Drives sloping correctly, no standing
water

_____ Loose concrete cleaned up, hauled off

_____ Steps sloped away from home

_____ Splash blocks below downspouts

_____ Approach installed correctly

_____ Water meter elevation correct

_____ Curbing and walks repaired, replaced
where necessary

Initial	Exterior finish

_____ All exterior trim installed properly

_____ Paint completed, masking cleaned up

_____ Windows and overspray cleaned

_____ Shutters installed securely

_____ Rain gutters installed correctly

_____ Shingles installed correctly

_____ Ridge cap installed correctly

_____ Chimney cap installed correctly

_____ Flashings caulked and sealed with plastic
cement

_____ Roof vents installed correctly

_____ Heating vent caps installed correctly

_____ Roof jacks caulked or sealed with plastic
cement

_____ Windows caulked securely including top

_____ Screens installed correctly

_____ Siding nailed properly with galvanized
nails

_____ Trim nailed, caulked properly

_____ Deck installed, nailed properly, painted

_____ Steps and railings secured

_____ Spacing on deck less than 3/8 inch

_____ Sonotubes cleaned up

_____ Exterior locks working

_____ Exterior doors properly hung

_____ Weather stripping and threshold installed properly

_____ Garage doors properly installed and
operating correctly

_____ Painting drips or bare spots

_____ General site clean up

Figure 13. Final inspection (cont.)

Initial **Interior Finish**

_____ Doors hung and fit properly according to plan
_____ Door bunkers installed properly
_____ Base joints fit tightly
_____ All shelving installed with clips
_____ Shelf rods installed correctly
_____ Check for runs in paint
_____ Check chips or scratches in wall
_____ Adequate insulation properly installed in attic
_____ Attic access installed, insulated properly
_____ Outlets and switches installed, no holes in sheetrock
_____ Check lights and outlets for operation
_____ Windows cleaned
_____ Bath hardware securely installed
_____ Mirrors securely installed
_____ Shower rods and doors installed properly and caulked
_____ Tile installed, cleaned, caulked

Initial

_____ Linoleum installed, caulked against tub or shower
_____ Plumbing fixtures installed with no leaks and working
_____ Appliances installed, working properly
_____ Counter tops installed, properly caulked where needed
_____ Rails and banisters securely fastened and stained
_____ Cabinets properly installed
_____ Cabinet doors and drawers operate properly
_____ Cabinet trim properly installed
_____ Check for scratches or dings in base and doors
_____ Floor coverings properly installed
_____ Linoleum seams sealed
_____ Carpet seams tight
_____ General interior clean up
_____ Basement cleanup, floor washed

_____

(Signature)

4

Budget Control

Introduction

Getting a project in at the established budget is a primary goal of every superintendent. Therefore, every project should have an established budget before a single nail is hammered—or even ordered. This budget may be determined from the estimate, or from accounting records (if the same type of house has been built previously). The budget should be subdivided into smaller categories, so that corrective action can be taken whenever budgeted and actual values differ. Corrective action may be in the form of some procedural or personnel change, or simply a recognition that the budget is in error and needs to be adjusted on future jobs.

Establishing the Budget

When choosing a method for subdividing the overall budget, you and other personnel involved will want to consider both the sophistication of the company and the kinds of homes being built, among other things. For example, different work areas may be grouped as follows:

- job overhead
- sitework
- footings and slabs
- masonry
- wood framing
- plumbing
- cabinets
- roofing and flash-ing
- electrical
- heating and air conditioning
- drywall
- interior wood trim
- painting
- floor covering
- appliances
- landscaping, walks, and drive-ways

Depending upon your company's needs, a chart of accounts may be used. Some examples of chart of account entries include construction materials inventory, maintenance and repair expense, and field office expenses. The complete NAHB Chart of Accounts is found in NAHB's *Accounting and Financial Management for Builders*.

In deciding how to subdivide the work areas, keep in mind that expenditures for each work item must be easily measurable. Another good rule is to lump together similar items that occur within the same time frame. For example, it would not be wise to put rough grading and finish grading together, since comparisons against the budget need to be made as quickly as possible after each work item is begun to see if the job is in keeping with the targeted budget. This advance warning system will often allow you to take corrective steps before it's too late.

You will want to work with office staff to ensure that the numbers used in accounting and budgeting procedures are as accurate as possible. Many building companies employ an integrated numbering system for accounting, estimating, purchasing, and other functions. Maintaining accurate time sheets relative to each work category and keeping up with materials moved from one job to another are essential to determining whether or not a job is profitable.

Material Control

In order to control the budget, you must take pains to control the materials used in the construction of homes. Proper utilization of materials is crucial to any construction company's cost-effective operation and is therefore an important superintendent responsibility. Material control is a function of seven basic building activities:

- Value engineering and planning
- Completing specifications
- Ensuring accurate contracts

- Purchasing
- Scheduling deliveries
- Providing proper storage and care of materials
- Avoiding material waste and misuse

Introduction to Value Engineering

In the home building industry, value engineering is an effort to get the most for consumers' dollars without sacrificing quality or the function for which the building is intended. The basis for value engineering in the industry centers on optimum value engineering (OVE) systems, such as the system developed in conjunction with the U.S. Department of Housing and Urban Development and the NAHB Research Center.

OVE systems offer many useful—and money-saving—guidelines for the utilization and conservation of materials. In addition, when OVE principles are applied systematically and appropriately, they produce a better product as well as a more economical one—one that serves its function better in many cases than a house built in a more traditional manner. For example, studies have shown that by placing studs and floor joists 24 inches on center and aligning them with the roof trusses (which are normally 24 inches on center), not only are materials conserved, but the structural stability of the building is increased (Figure 14).

As mentioned earlier, OVE is a group of closely related cost-saving methods. It begins during the planning process, takes into account alternate construction techniques, and is carefully integrated with the construction process so that all phases of construction effectively complement each other. While OVE techniques do not require detailed engineering analysis, professional engineering advice may sometimes prove helpful in making the most of OVE concepts. Having an engineer design or evaluate each house, however, is unnecessary; concepts that prove valid in one instance can be applied in similar situations on other jobs.

Value Engineering: Four Steps

Value engineering is based upon the following four simple steps:

- Gathering information
- Speculating on alternatives
- Analyzing and evaluating alternatives
- Selecting and implementing the best alternatives

Gathering Information. First, the worth of an item used in construction should be determined in dollar amounts. However, in some cases, an item may have aesthetic value but little or no structural value.

The value must then be determined by the individual purchasing the product. For example, a home buyer may wish to have a certain type of window placed in his or her home out of personal preference, perhaps because the window is particularly attractive. This type of consideration is entirely different from purchasing windows to achieve energy efficiency.

Speculating on Alternatives. This speculation involves generating new, cost-saving ideas and concepts to serve necessary functions within the house being built. For example, many new, innovative approaches currently focus on efficient floor plans and products that make the most of fewer square feet while producing a home that meets the needs of potential buyers.

Analyzing and Evaluating Alternatives. This analysis step should be both systematic and objective. In order to determine the advantages and disadvantages of an alternative approach, each must be evaluated and tested to ensure feasibility. To estimate an alternative's value, ask: What does it cost overall, and what are the potential savings? Other factors you should consider when evaluating alternatives include aesthetics, durability, marketability, and lifetime cost with maintenance (as distinct from unit-in-place cost).

Selecting and Implementing Alternatives. Once the alternatives have been evaluated, some ideas will fail to meet a building's operating or functional requirements and will be rejected outright. Other alternatives may appear to have great potential but require additional information before reaching a final decision; such alternatives should be reserved for further research. Finally, those ideas offering the greatest savings, while still maintaining the functional qualities required, should be selected for implementation. Once a final decision has been reached, all costs should be recorded and monitored, including installation, maintenance, and use of the product or technique, to ensure that the anticipated savings are realized.

Completing Specifications

Specifications can be a superintendent's worst nightmare. You may be provided with only a foundation plan, floor plan, and elevation and asked to construct a house from this sketchy information. Proper use of adequate plans and specifications can eliminate most problems before they begin. By clarifying the homeowner's wants (in the case of custom work) and completing the specifications, builders and superintendents can improve efficiency on

Figure 14. Comparison of 16-inch and 24-inch on-center framing

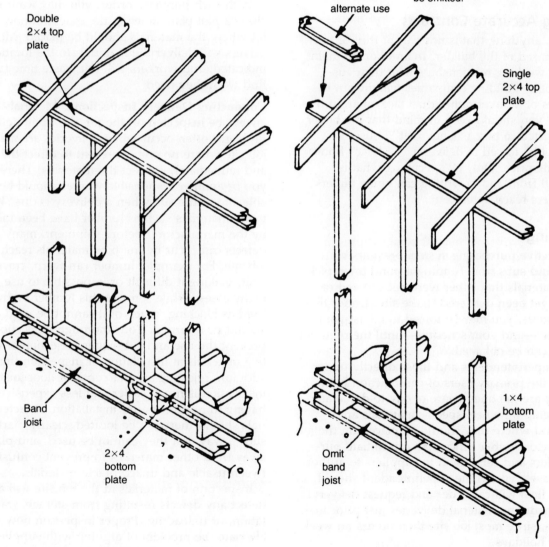

**Standard framing
16 inches on center**
Truss, stud, and joist may
or may not be in line.

Double
2×4 top
plate

Band
joist

2×4
bottom
plate

**OVE framing
24 inches on center**
Truss, stud, and joist are
directly in line. Load is
supplied more efficiently.
In addition to savings on top
and bottom plates and band
joist, structural headers may
be omitted.

1×4 on 2×4
alternate use

Single
2×4 top
plate

1×4
bottom
plate

Omit
band
joist

the job site and make intelligent, accurate decisions when submitting bids for custom work. Therefore, regardless who furnishes the plans and specifications, make certain that every item is specified or that at least an allowance is agreed upon. When setting these allowances, many building companies recommend values that are too low in order to make the overall price more attractive. However, setting realistic values for allowances initially helps keep the home buyer happy—minimizing the possibility of surprises, and their accompanying higher costs, later. This professional approach will help to keep your company's good reputation intact as well.

Ensuring Accurate Contracts

Legally, anything that is not part of the contract is not required of the builder. In an effort to maintain good working relationships with their customers, many building companies will give in to the wishes of a buyer rather than face an argument. However, you should keep in mind that if a buyer has contracted to buy a "Chevrolet" house, you should not be forced to deliver a "Cadillac" house at the same price. Only by specifying what is wanted up front and in writing can home buyers and builders reach agreement.

Purchasing

An effective purchasing system prevents your workers and subs from running around town picking up materials that either were not ordered or have not yet been delivered to the site. Under these circumstances, you may be forced to adjust your labor crews—and your schedule—until the required materials can be obtained.

Since superintendents and those directly under them are the primary users of construction materials, they are the ones aware of day-to-day material needs, including where specific materials are needed and where they should be placed on the job site. Therefore, while office staff can initiate purchase orders and send them to suppliers to authorize purchases, you as the superintendent should place the final will-call order and request delivery. Avoid scheduling material deliveries just prior to weekends, since most job site theft occurs on weekends and holidays.

Scheduling Deliveries

Most of what you need to know about scheduling deliveries is basic common sense: materials should be delivered when they are needed and stored close to where they will be used. Proper scheduling of material deliveries cuts down on both wasted time and wasted materials.

Have a Specified Delivery Site. Identifying each building site with a conspicuous number, and putting that same number on all delivery tickets, helps to ensure that materials arrive at the correct location. You should make certain that delivered materials are stacked with the materials to be used first on top of the pile. One way to accomplish this arrangement is to list those items required on top of the pile at the *bottom* of the purchase order. These materials will likely be loaded onto the truck last and therefore end up on the top of the pile.

With each purchase order, you may want to include a plot plan showing the exact location on the lot where the materials should be placed. Most drivers will deliver the materials to the location indicated, and workers will not waste time trying to find what they need.

Conducting Delivery Inspections. Materials should always be inspected on the job site upon delivery. Problems often occur when deliveries are made to a job site where no one is present to direct the driver and immediately inspect the materials. Therefore, you or another responsible worker should be available and at the site when a delivery is due. While many materials such as lumber have been inspected by the manufacturer before shipment, many latent defects can occur by the time materials reach the job site. For example, lumber can warp, crack, and split, making it difficult or impossible to use in many cases. While some of this lumber might be used as blocking, much of it cannot be used and should be returned. Your thorough inspection can prevent the use and subsequent rejection of defective materials at installation or inspection time. In addition, rejecting an unacceptable floor joist before installation is much easier and less expensive than having to replace it after installation. Rejected materials should therefore be located, clearly marked in such a way that they cannot be used, and placed away from other materials to prevent confusion between usable and unacceptable materials.

Inspection of materials at the job site will also detect any defects resulting from storage, transportation, or unloading. Proper inspection now will alleviate the problem of arguing with suppliers later over any damage. You should keep in mind that suppliers are often the victims of unjust claims for defective materials when, in fact, the problem occurred as a result of product misuse or abuse on the part of the superintendent or workers during construction. Suppliers have consequently become more sensitive about complaints from superintendents about damaged materials. Inspection upon delivery should limit the room for argument on both sides.

Most suppliers are honest and will not intentionally short a builder. However, employees are human and often forget a particular item or leave materials back at the warehouse instead of delivering them to the job site. This problem is common for small items such as nails, bolts, and adhesive, particularly in large orders where items are easily overlooked. Therefore, inspect carefully to ensure all materials have been delivered as ordered.

Finally, you should always be conscious of your right and your obligation to reject faulty materials. Most material suppliers will stand behind their products and substitute good materials for inferior ones, usually at no cost to you.

Providing Proper Storage and Care

Materials on the job site are often wasted because of improper storage and care. For example, materials can be ruined by mud or snow during extreme weather conditions. In the hot weather common in many parts of the country, exposed lumber can dry out and warp; when shipped to hot, dry climates, even kiln-dried lumber can be ruined through careless storage—or lack of storage. Materials subject to deterioration should therefore be covered at all times. In addition, a bundle of lumber should be used as soon as possible after it is opened to prevent warping and twisting. Twenty guidelines for the conservation and care of building materials, prepared by Lee Evans in his *Quality in Construction*, are offered in Figure 15.

Avoiding Material Waste and Misuse

The large scrap piles found on most construction sites are the most obvious symptom of the growing problem of material waste in the construction industry. Taking the time to preplan your use of materials can eliminate a substantial amount of this waste. Spend a little extra time at the drafting table and graphically depict how materials are to be installed. The resulting drawings can communicate to your workers and subs the exact manner in which materials are to be used—eliminating waste and saving money. Many building companies also distribute copies of approved construction methods and procedures, further stipulating efficient material utilization.

Labor Control

Many builders feel they have little control over materials, focusing instead on labor costs as the primary avenue for potential savings. Granted, this greater labor control may have been true in the past when builders did a large portion of their work with their own labor. However, with the recent trend in homebuilding toward the increased use of subcontractors, labor efficiency no longer directly affects the cost of the job. Of course, the superintendent who discovers ways for a subcontractor to increase productivity may lower costs for future jobs. In addition, you can help to keep costs down by watching carefully for subcontractor errors that may be properly backcharged to the responsible sub.

Figure 15. Guidelines for conservation and care of building materials*

    1. Can materials be ordered in smaller quantities to reduce exposure time?

    2. Can the supplier load them so that materials used first are on the top instead of the bottom of the load? (Because of the time saved builders may be able to afford to pay something extra for this service, especially if they use their own crews or can negotiate with subcontractors to recover some of the time savings.)

    3. Can the superintendent do anything else to improve planning load composition, size, or delivery spotting to avoid extra handling?

    4. Can any kind of temporary cover such as plastic be used? (Provide shelter but do not make a sweat box by covering materials too tightly.)

    5. Can the load be banded in several batches rather than in one big lot?

    6. Is a spot by the foundation prepared for the load? Does it provide drainage? Are skids provided to keep the load off the ground? (Ideally it should be up six inches, and in bad weather, polyethylene laid below the load to prevent moisture rise.)

    7. Are asphalt roofing materials stored flat? (Curved and buckled shingles create an unsightly roof.)

    8. Can any of the load delivery spots be covered with stone or paved? In multifamily projects paving or stone is desirable because subsequent handling can be done with lift trucks, but doing that requires much planning and scheduling.)

    9. Are siding materials stored so that they will not be scratched or damaged?

   10. Can scheduling be changed to prevent deliveries from being exposed to weather for more than a day or two?

   11. Can theft of site materials be reduced? Can they be nailed down or locked up before dark? Will reducing deliveries to one-day requirements help? Can materials be banded or wired or nailed together to prevent quick pick-ups? Can materials ends or sides be painted with an odd-color spray paint to help recover materials or identify them for prosecution? Can superintendents and builders do anything in the way of rewards for information by banding together?

   12. What can be done to prevent vandalism?

   13. Can superintendents train in-house labor and subcontractor workers to take better care of materials? (Stacks that are torn into and scattered deteriorate rapidly.)

   14. Is too much material ordered for a particular unit or building resulting in waste, downgrading, or rehandling?

   15. Is a place prepared for temporary storage of trim and similar materials so that they are dry, straight, and not disturbed?

   16. Is each unit dried-in quickly enough? Is siding applied soon enough to prevent water damage in the house?

   17. Is temporary drainage directed away from the house provided?

   18. Can some deliveries and phases of construction be rescheduled so that materials are not damaged by workers? (For example, lay flooring materials late in the process. Don't deliver doors, door frames, and windows until the unit is ready for their installation. These items as well as walls and finishes are damaged when workers move them.)

   19. Can protective coverings be provided for such items as bathtubs, flooring materials, plastic laminate tops, and appliances?

   20. Can temporary furnace heat be provided to help dry out the house and to prevent moisture build-up in flooring materials, trim, and paneling?

---

* Adapted from Lee S. Evans, *Quality in Construction* (Washington, D.C.: National Association of Home Builders, 1974), p. 51.

5

Schedule Control

Introduction

Getting a job completed according to the established schedule is another primary goal of the superintendent. With all the interrelated functions that must be accomplished in proper sequence, construction must progress in the most efficient and economical manner possible. Effective scheduling is the key to this efficiency and contributes directly to the success of many builders in today's competitive marketplace.

Basically, a good schedule allows you to build a house with less effort, because a formal, written schedule organizes the work sequence in much the same way a good set of plans organizes what is to be built. Because a formal schedule makes the work easier, more houses can often be built than was possible using informal scheduling.

Why Schedule?

Many builders and superintendents who currently "fly by the seat of their pants" may wonder why they need to adopt a more formal scheduling approach. The reasons are many:

- Scheduling can help to level out the up-and-down cycles typical to the construction industry by reducing slack time and increasing overall productivity.
- Scheduling should point out bottlenecks where labor, equipment, and materials are spread too thin.
- Scheduling can alleviate problems of crews with insufficient work.
- Scheduling provides options when unexpected delays occur due to equipment breakdowns, subcontractors failing to show up, or bad weather. Flexibility in work assignments is also improved.

Getting Started

It is possible for a superintendent to use a schedule effectively without being able to draw one. However, knowing how to create a formal schedule on paper should help you to use and understand the schedule even better. Since the intent of this chapter is to enable you to use a schedule effectively, many of the steps necessary to creating a schedule are provided. Superintendents and builders interested in learning more about formal scheduling procedures should see *Scheduling for Builders* from the National Association of Home Builders.

Scheduling Methods

The type of scheduling system a building company uses depends on several interrelated factors:

- size of building company
- volume of work accomplished
- type of construction
- owner or architect's requirements (in custom work)
- project location
- competition
- project size
- project complexity
- extent of subcontracted work
- capacity of the superintendent
- work load (current and anticipated)
- past experience with schedules
- contract provisions
- time available

While many scheduling methods are in use in the construction industry today, including many computer applications, this discussion will concentrate on two of the most practical for either manual or computer use: the bar chart and the Critical Path Method (CPM) diagram.

Scheduling Phases

There are three distinct phases to formal scheduling for both the bar chart and CPM methods:

- Planning: different activities are broken out, and their relationships to one another are determined.
- Scheduling: the time required to perform each activity is determined, and those activities with slack time are determined.
- Monitoring: the superintendent uses the written schedule to organize the work.

Sequencing Activities

Work should flow without interruption. To achieve this flow, activities must be properly sequenced from the start. You should particularly keep in mind that two or more distinct parts of a particular task occurring at different times in the job need to be scheduled as separate activities. For example, the electrical work should be divided into electrical rough-in and electrical trim-out.

Activities are technically defined as "a single work step that has a recognizable beginning and end and requires time for its accomplishment." As you consider the various construction activities, you may want to organize them according to the following categories:

- Area of responsibility or craft: Each subcontractor should be represented by at least one activity, and by more than one activity if they are performing work at different stages.
- Structural elements: Activities using the same subcontractor, such as footings and concrete flatwork, may be separated since they represent different structural elements.
- Location on project: Similar activities, such as interior concrete, floors, and exterior flatwork may be considered separate activities because they are performed in different locations, usually at different times.
- Material vendor: Materials supplied by different vendors, such as garage doors and interior doors, should usually be considered separate activities.

Your final activities list should be arranged in sequential order. Three crucial questions should be answered in order to develop an accurate sequence:

- Which activities must precede this activity?
- Which activities must follow this activity?
- Which activities can be conducted simultaneously?

Several constraints can also affect sequence, including the following:

- Physical (or logical) constraints: Physical constraints involve such factors as labor and/or equipment availability, construction methods, and safety constraints.
- Practical constraints: Practical constraints are either an economic or safety consideration: What is the safest, most economical way to accomplish a task? Failure to consider such constraints can be disastrous to an otherwise adequate job schedule.
- Managerial constraints: Management may require that a project be constructed in a specific way. Such constraints may be a direct result of the homebuyer's desires, the company's financial requirements, computer or accounting constraints, the availability of competent managerial control, or simply managerial preference. These constraints are real, and you should be prepared to work within the guidelines established.

Determining Activity Duration

Assigning the time required for construction activities is usually based on experience and knowledge of local conditions. You should begin by obtaining a time estimate from each subcontractor. Sometimes, busy subs may move onto a job and "stake a claim" while doing little work, then move off the job to finish or start another job. A good estimate of time requirements up front should help to curtail this behavior.

Several rules will help you in estimating activity durations:

- Evaluate each activity independent of all others.
- Obtain information from subcontractors on time durations.
- Assume a normal work force for your company. Avoid overloading your work force to make the activity duration match the overall time allotted.
- Assume normal production rates.
- Assume a normal work day. Overtime or multiple-shift work can be entered into the process later if needed. While a certain portion of the work may be accelerated for a limited time to meet a crisis or solve a particular problem, this solution should be the exception rather than the rule.
- Use consistent time units of working days and half days.

- Be as accurate as is practicable. Do not overestimate time durations in an attempt to make the schedule more manageable, or underestimate in order to keep it tight.

A good rule to follow: no activity should be scheduled for less than half a day. Any task taking less time should be rounded up to a half day. For example, to get to a job and set the grade stakes may take only an hour, but a half day should be scheduled. Likewise, any activity that is expected to take five or six hours, such as grading the lot, should be scheduled as a whole day.

The Bar Chart

Planning the Bar Chart

The bar chart is the more basic of the two scheduling methods offered here, requiring only that all construction activities be sequenced, and that a time duration be estimated for each.

Scheduling with the Bar Chart

A bar chart puts construction activities in a calendar format. Figure 16 shows a complete list of activities with projected time slots. The bars on the calendar portion of the chart indicate when the activities are to occur. According to this sample chart, the house should be completed in thirty working days.

One of the biggest advantages to a bar chart is its simple visual presentation. When an activity will begin and end is easily seen and understood. You and your workers and subs can see at a glance how the work will progress.

Monitoring the Bar Chart

Unfortunately, the strengths of the bar chart method can also become weaknesses when monitoring activities. For example, a bar chart cannot show the complex interdependence between various activities. Therefore, you may wish to reserve the bar chart method for use as a general planning tool when a graphic display of the interrelationships is unnecessary.

The Critical Path Diagram

Unlike the bar chart method, the Critical Path Method of scheduling identifies those activities that *must* be completed on schedule in order for the job to finish on time.

Planning the CPM Diagram

When planning a CPM diagram, the sequencing and duration activities are much the same as those for a bar chart. The difference is in how the CPM diagram relates activities' sequence and duration to each other. In a CPM diagram, an arrow represents work, and a circle (or node) represents a point in time (see Figure 17). Each circle contains a number identifying each activity. For example, activity 17-19 represents "hang and finish drywall."

Scheduling with a CPM Diagram

Following a CPM diagram is relatively simple. A basic rule states that *all* arrows coming into the start of a particular activity must be completed before that activity can begin. For example, on our sample house shown in Figure 17, it was determined that wood trim and cabinets would be installed before ceramic tile is begun. Another important rule relates to dashed (or "dummy") arrows, such as the arrow from 8 to 9. While no work is represented by the dashed arrow, all work coming into the dashed arrow must be completed before the work *after* the dashed arrow can commence. For example, the dashed arrow from 8 to 9 shows that brick work may begin only after masonry materials have been delivered, water is at the site, and framing is complete.

Applying the above rules throughout the sample CPM diagram, you can follow the superintendent's scheduling approach. First, the scheduler determines and schedules the first job: obtaining the building permit. With the permit in hand, rough grading may be done. After the grading is complete, three tasks can begin:

- Temporary power may be brought to the site.
- Water may be brought to the site.
- Bricks may be delivered.

Notice that after the framing is completed (6-7), the plumbing top out, HVAC rough-in, electrical rough-in, and roofing may be done. Also notice that when these three jobs have been completed, the walls may be insulated (13-15) and a general clean-up planned (13-14).

Monitoring the CPM Diagram

It is in the monitoring phase that the superintendent can use the CPM diagram to greatest advantage. One of the most effective monitoring techniques involves highlighting activities or parts of activities with a colored pen or highlighter. By doing so, you will be able to tell at a glance which

Figure 16. Bar chart

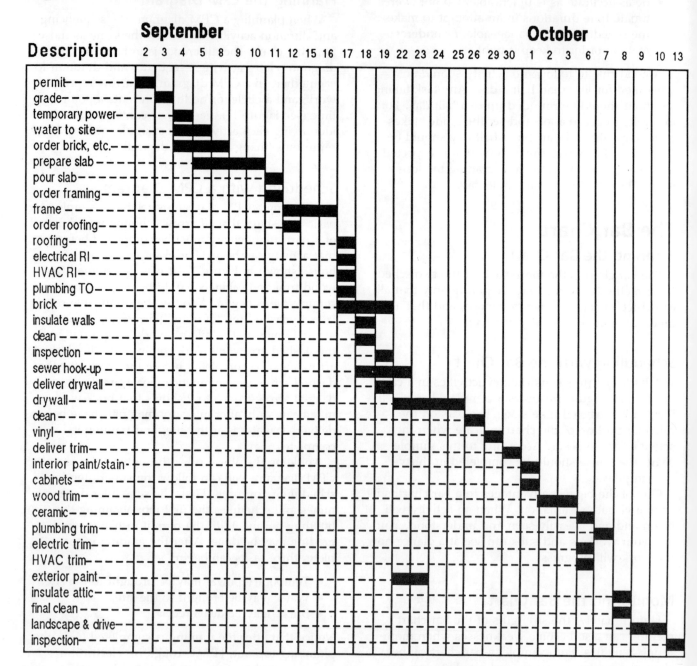

Figure 17. CPM diagram for a house

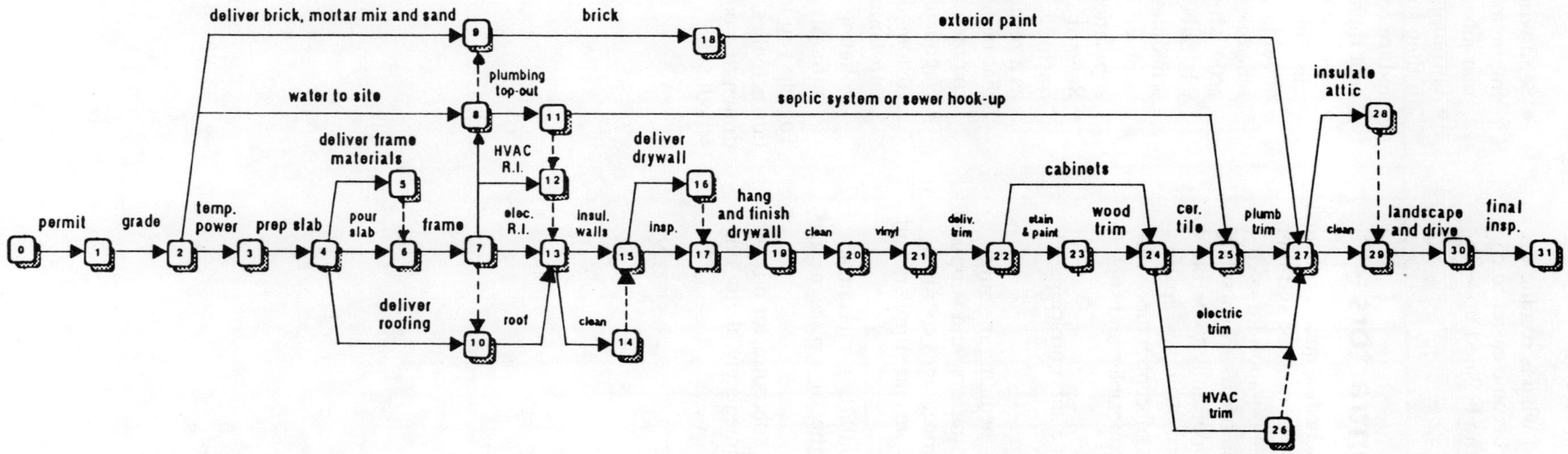

activities are under way—and what is coming up next. Material deliveries will become easier to control. Finally, subcontractors can be lined up with greater reliability.

Scheduling Subcontractors

The only accurate way to schedule subcontractors is to first consult with each subcontractor and then negotiate a mutually agreeable duration for each activity. Resistance most often occurs when subcontractors are not offered an opportunity to participate in the scheduling process. Such participation should substantially improve subcontractors' willingness to establish realistic timetables and stick to them.

Several key points relate to a subcontractor's schedule:

- Hold a preconstruction scheduling meeting with all key staff, subcontractors, and suppliers involved. This meeting encourages coordination between subcontractors and suppliers and eliminates bottlenecks.
- Avoid scheduling two conflicting subcontractors on the same job, in the same place, at the same time.
- Have a job ready for the subcontractor on schedule; notify them immediately of any unavoidable delays.

- Send written notices to subcontractors reminding them when they are scheduled for a particular job.
- Encourage cooperation among subcontractors. If they suggest good, practical ideas on how to reduce cost or time and maintain quality, accept them.
- Base payment on compliance with the schedule. Subcontractors adhering to the schedule should be paid on time; if they delay the schedule, delay their checks to correspond exactly with the number of days they delayed the job. Subcontractors soon get the message when schedules are tied to checks. Interest may be imposed or penalty payments assessed if this stipulation is not included in the contract.
- Reward superior performance. If the subcontractor is responsible for a substantial savings as a result of superior performance, reward that performance with a bonus and a letter of commendation.
- Negotiate with subcontractors who are not accustomed to working under a tight schedule. Substantial time savings can be realized by negotiating from a position of knowledge and authority.

To help you in visualizing the timing of construction activities, Figure 18 provides a CPM diagram drawn to a time scale showing when each activity is scheduled.

Figure 18. CPM diagram drawn to a time scale

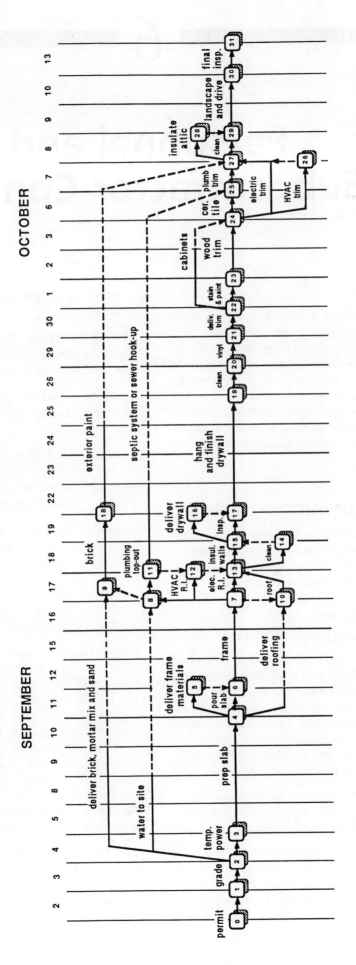

49

6

Personnel and Subcontractor Control

Introduction

Not so many years ago, a construction company's reputation was often based on the skill of the craftspersons on its payroll. In those days, skilled workers were a tremendous asset, and construction companies often did a large majority of their work, if not all, with their hourly forces. The trend in residential construction in recent years has shifted toward subcontracting more and more of the job, with some companies subcontracting all of the work.

Hired Labor or Subcontractor?

Many factors enter into the decision to use hired labor forces or subcontractors for a particular construction job. You should weigh the advantages and disadvantages carefully before reaching a decision.

Advantages of Using Subcontractors

Greater Flexibility. The demand for new homes fluctuates greatly, particularly in relation to current mortgage interest rates. In times of high demand, building companies like to build as many homes as possible; when demand is low, they usually choose to slow the pace. The more a building company relies on subcontractors, the easier it will be to achieve this increased or decreased output.

Less Risk. By subcontracting work, building companies transfer some of the financial, employment, and management risks to the subcontractor.

Less Capital Investment. Subcontractors often furnish material, labor, tools, and equipment. In these cases, the building company can reduce its capital investment by paying subcontractors only upon completion of their work and only at regular intervals.

Less Bookkeeping. Because the builder requires fewer employees and purchases fewer materials, less bookkeeping is usually required.

Less Waste. When subcontractors supply their own materials, damage and waste tend to be kept to a minimum.

Less Overhead. By using subcontractors, builders do not need to purchase, rent, or maintain nearly as much equipment. In addition, with fewer employees, tax and insurance costs are reduced.

Improved Quality. Subcontractors usually specialize in one or two particular trades and become skillful and efficient in them. Therefore, the quality of work is easier to control. If builders establish acceptable quality standards prior to the start of work, they can usually ensure this quality by withholding payment until those standards are met.

Improved Scheduling. Because subcontractors are independent, a builder can stipulate in the contract that certain schedules be followed and that penalties will be imposed for noncompliance. One Chicago builder has used a "progressive network," a system requiring each subcontractor to notify the next one when his or her job is complete and the next step can begin. For this type of system to work successfully, you will need good working relationships with all your subcontractors. Additionally, the notification requirement must be included in the subcontractor agreement.

Less-Detailed Supervision. Superintendents are usually not required to supervise subcontractor's day-to-day activities, since subcontractors are responsible for their own work.

Disadvantages of Using Subcontractors

More Coordination. The superintendent has a much greater coordination burden when working with subcontractors. Making last-minute schedule changes can also prove difficult.

Unqualified Subcontractors. Because of the low capital investment usually required, starting a subcontracting business is fairly easy. Many states do not require either a license or experience, resulting in subcontractors who may not be qualified to handle a job in terms of knowledge, experience, or adequate financing.

Supply and Demand. In good economic times when demand for housing is high, a sufficient supply of subcontractors may not be available. The few subcontractors willing to take on more work may be overextended and unable to meet all of their commitments.

Experienced Supervision Required. Superintendents must be qualified to distinguish high quality work from substandard work. They must be prepared to recognize problems immediately, suggest alternatives, and converse intelligently with those involved in the trades.

Subcontractor Control

Once you have evaluated your needs carefully and made the decision to hire one or more subcontractors to perform work on a project, you will need to consider the qualities you require in a subcontractor, and then begin your search.

Qualities of a Good Subcontractor

- financial stability
- quality workmanship
- cost-consciousness
- ability to stay on schedule
- dependability
- cooperation
- adequate work force
- prompt payment of bills
- prompt service on call-backs
- ability to conduct business in a professional manner
- awareness of material waste
- adequate insurance coverage
- adequate employee supervision
- fair prices

The Subcontractor/Superintendent Relationship

A cooperative relationship between subcontractor and superintendent is a vital aspect of a successful construction business. You should therefore encourage subcontractors to suggest new products, materials, or techniques. A subcontractor's comprehensive knowledge of new products in a particular craft can often result in savings for both parties.

While a subcontractor works for the building company in a relationship similar to that of an employee, the subcontractor is *not* the builder's employee. Their relationship is established by means of a written contract. Because the builder is the contractor, and the subcontractor the contractee, the former should stipulate the terms of any contract.

Always keep in mind that a subcontractor must make a fair profit in order to stay in business. Builders and their superintendents should be careful not to take advantage of subcontractors who are inexperienced or who have made an obvious mistake in their estimating. These subcontractors may get the job for a cheap price, but you can probably count on work that is just as cheap. Disqualifying ridiculously low bids, or even giving a subcontractor the opportunity to back out gracefully, is usually better.

Locating Subcontractors

The best subcontractors are usually the busiest ones. To find good ones, building companies should contact their local home builders association, other builders, and other superintendents to find out which subcontractors they prefer. Inspectors can also be excellent sources of information on subcontractor competence, since they see every subcontractor's work and are often in the best position to compare subs fairly to one another.

You can get a pretty good idea of how a subcontractor performs by inspecting other projects. Consider the following questions as you examine the site:

- Is the job clean?
- Is the quality good?
- Does the job sit for long periods without much progress?
- Are sufficient workers on the job to get it done, or does the job appear to move too slowly?
- How do the workers treat visitors?

Finally, check each potential subcontractor's current financial status with material suppliers (be sure to check with more than one) and credit bureaus.

Managing Subcontractors

As the superintendent, you must have the managerial ability to schedule, coordinate, and control all subcontractors on your job(s) so that work proceeds—as always—on schedule, within the established budget, and according to the quality specified. In addition, you will need to evaluate the managerial abilities of each subcontractor and determine if the subcontractor will be able to meet payrolls and overhead costs, pay suppliers, and still make a profit. Building companies in even the best financial condition may find themselves in difficult circumstances if subcontractors go broke in the middle of a job. Because the building industry is so dynamic and volatile, some builders have been seriously hurt by irresponsible subcontractors.

The Superintendent's Role

Your managerial role changes when subcontractors are used. Instead of being responsible for motivating and coordinating your own work forces, you must direct and control highly independent subcontractors, who in turn direct their own crews. You should therefore try to foster cooperation between subcontractors, particularly when their needs conflict, and mediate an acceptable resolution when necessary.

You can make the supervisory task a smoother one by ensuring that jobs are ready when a subcontractor arrives. Subcontractors are often called in too early, resulting in costly extra trips. Subcontractors should be given as much lead time as possible to facilitate their scheduling and avoid last-minute decision-making. In addition, every superintendent should inspect subcontractors' work in a timely manner so that any necessary changes can be made with minimal delay and expense.

Written Contracts

A wise man once said, "An oral contract is not worth the paper it's written on," and it is true that oral agreements can be difficult to enforce when disagreements occur. Yet many builders and superintendents continue to operate on a promise and a handshake for the following reasons:

- Unfamiliarity with contract provisions and law.
- Reluctance of subcontractors to be bound by written agreements.

- Lack of standard contract procedures in many building companies.
- Ability of most subcontractors to perform adequately without a contract.

Written contracts spell out a subcontractor's exact requirements and thus eliminate many areas of potential disagreement. Provisions to include in every subcontract agreement include the following:

- plans and specifications
- policies and procedures
- scheduling requirements
- change order routines
- warranties and customer service
- penalties for failure to meet contractual provisions.
- other general conditions, such as use of facilities, payment terms, inspection requirements, and quality of work.

Plans and Specifications. Specifications must define as clearly as possible exactly what is intended in easily understandable terms of the trade. Occasionally, residential construction plans are superficial documents that don't begin to cover all of the important details. Poor specifications lacking a clear definition of how the house is to be built will confuse and frustrate subcontractors. If superintendents and builders are not familiar with the options and alternatives available, they should consult specialists to establish the detailed specifications that will meet their needs and eliminate guesswork. Any additions or changes to the plans and specifications should be properly authorized and submitted with accompanying change orders.

Policies and Procedures. Policies establish the philosophy of how a company will conduct business. Procedures, on the other hand, stipulate the exact manner in which business will be conducted. Establishing policies and procedures for both running a business and completing a job is one of the first steps a building company must take to prevent problems, avoid disagreements, and eliminate confusion. Policies and procedures for a building company might include the following, listed in approximate order of importance:

- scope of work to be performed
- lines of authority and channels of communication
- acceptance of materials on the job
- proper conduct on the job
- use of site facilities
- acceptable and unacceptable construction methods

- use of equipment, materials, and temporary utilities
- provision of adequate crews on the job
- compliance with schedules
- safety and accident procedures
- protection of other subcontractors' work
- acceptance of the work
- payment policies and procedures
- lien protection requirements
- liability and other insurance coverage
- clean-up procedures
- call-back and warranty procedures
- special exceptions

These standard policies and procedures can be outlined as a separate document and simply referred to and included in the subcontract provisions along with the plans and specifications. They should be stated in a positive manner and should not be merely a collection of "thou shalt nots."

Scheduling

Scheduling subcontractors is normally the superintendent's responsibility (see Chapter 5, "Schedule Control"). To expedite construction, a work schedule must be coordinated with each subcontractor. This schedule is often included as part of the contract documents to ensure the subcontractor's commitment. Progress meetings can also help in coordinating the smooth flow of construction operations.

A superintendent's positive action, particularly at the early scheduling stage, can prevent many complaints. Matters likely to create controversy should be decided as far in advance as possible, with the resulting decisions communicated to all superintendents and subcontractors. The superintendent can then spend less time arguing and more time seeing that work gets done.

Change Orders

Change orders tend to be a source of frequent disagreement if handled improperly. Keeping accurate records on every requested change is extremely important. Therefore, every change request should be documented through a formal change order procedure, including the following:

- request for change order
- change order cost estimate
- schedule update
- written approval signed by both parties
- change order deposit or payment
- completion of the requested change

Obviously, the cost of the change order, as well as

any increased costs related to rescheduling, should be passed on to the party requesting the change.

Warranties and Customer Service

Customer service is one of the primary sources of homeowner complaints against builders. Most buyers are satisfied with their homes on settlement day but become disappointed later when something goes wrong or they attempt to correct a mistake after move-in. The superintendent's frustration is compounded when he or she is unable to motivate the appropriate subcontractor to handle customer service calls in a timely manner. You can eliminate a great deal of confusion, delay, and frustration by stipulating subcontractors' customer service and warranty requirements in their contracts, including the time limits permitted. More detailed information on working with the buyer is included in Chapter 7.

The Dangers of Familiarity

Although building companies often find it easier to deal with the same subcontractors on numerous jobs, the builder and superintendent must determine the relative importance of price, service, quality, and management complexity as they relate to subcontracting. Building companies should avoid taking on additional costs merely to simplify subcontractor management.

If a building company does decide to use the same subcontractors over time on several jobs, superintendents must continue to check regularly to ensure all subcontractors are remaining competitive and maintain the builder's standards of quality. When a superintendent, builder, and subcontractors become too friendly, there is the danger that each side may begin to take the other for granted, leading to problems. To counter these problems, some building companies request competitive bids on each job to keep their regular subcontractors honest. This practice ensures a competitive price, provides better control, and maintains a higher level of service. In addition, you may want to check your subcontractors' financial status occasionally to prevent problems as a result of changing economic winds.

Hired Personnel Control

When a building company chooses to perform the majority of its field work with its own hired personnel, rather than employing subcontractors, the superintendent's job changes markedly. You will be less concerned with coordinating various crafts and more concerned with planning work so that workers are kept busy for maximum productivity. The two superintendent functions essential to the success of personnel control are hiring and training.

The Nine Steps to Hiring Personnel

The following nine steps are crucial to effective hiring of construction personnel:

- Assess organizational needs
- Prepare job descriptions
- Assess current employees
- Follow effective recruiting practices
- Evaluate application forms and resumes
- Conduct the initial screening and interviews
- Check references
- Conduct final interviews
- Make a final selection

Assess Organizational Needs. Most builders and superintendents face hiring problems when they fail to define their needs clearly at the outset. Prior planning is therefore essential to effective hiring.

Many superintendents fall into the trap of looking at their wants, rather than their *needs*. These superintendents usually end up hiring persons similar to themselves, mistakenly assuming that persons like themselves are more likely to be successful. While having a protegé can certainly satisfy a superintendent's ego, hiring workers with substantially different, yet complementary, backgrounds will normally offer greater rewards in the long run. With so many different and diverse skills required in the construction industry, it only makes sense to hire someone who will add to the building organization, rather than fit an existing mold. For example, if personnel are currently available to estimate jobs but lack the ability to organize and schedule work, these attributes should be sought in new employees. On the other hand, if a building company has workers for framing and layout who are not as productive as they could be, you should look for a productive worker with qualities that will motivate others.

In assessing company needs, you will also want to do the following:

- Look at the competition. What type of workers make up their organizations?
- Seek the opinion of those within the company who will be working with the new employee(s).
- Talk to bankers and others who know the building industry in general, and your company in particular.
- Talk to subcontractors about any needs they see.

Prepare Job Descriptions. Once your company's needs have been clearly defined, job descriptions should be formulated to serve as checklists in assessing applicant qualifications and comparing them with the needs of the organization. These job descriptions should contain the following:

- all functions to be performed
- job responsibilities
- description of resources available
- description of the extent of authority
- description of relationships with other members of the organization.

A job description may already be available for many positions. However, if company needs require a new or revised position, a new job description should be prepared. In addition to technical or mechanical skills, you should emphasize the more general attributes and abilities the job requires, including:

- leadership skills
- organizational skills
- practical intelligence
- flexibility
- initiative to originate necessary action
- ability to confront problems and deal with unpleasant situations
- oral and written communication skills
- listening skills
- decisiveness and ability to take action
- ability to understand procedures and monitor processes and subordinates
- ability to control stress and maintain stable performance levels
- interpersonal sensitivity
- ability to learn and apply new information
- motivation for work
- necessary mathematical skills
- an understanding of space relationships, particularly in visualizing shapes from drawings.
- mechanical reasoning skills
- reading skills to comprehend written materials with speed and accuracy

A complete and accurate job description is one of the superintendent's best hiring guides and can be particularly helpful when evaluating individuals for promotions and pay increases.

Assess Current Employees. Experts in personnel management constantly stress the importance of promoting an organization's present employees whenever possible. This preference over outside recruiting is understandable given the riskiness of hiring new people. Promoting current employees minimizes this risk, since the odds of objectively evaluating their skills, abilities, and knowledge are greatly enhanced. In addition, an environment that offers employees the opportunity to grow within an organization is a healthier one: performance improves and turnover declines. Many large organizations have a policy that at least three people should be in training for each manager's job at all times. This policy gives continuity to the company and reduces the tendency toward "management by crisis."

Current employees should be evaluated according to the following criteria:

- Does the employee have a positive attitude toward work and himself or herself?
- Is the employee technically competent to do the job?
- Does the employee understand the complexity of the business and the role the job has in the company's profitable operation?
- Does the employee have a good record of attendance?
- Does the employee look for ways to become more productive—and make other employees and the job more productive?
- Is the employee loyal to the company, company management, and the building industry?
- Does the employee get along with others? Can the employee motivate others to maximum performance?
- Does the employee have the potential to continue growing with the company, or is the employee at or near a "level of incompetence"?

The extent to which current employees meet these criteria will determine how much recruiting will be necessary. If the requirements are met in their entirety, new prospects should not be needed. However, if current employees fail to meet the criteria sufficiently, you may want to recruit enough outside individuals to conduct a comparison of all available candidates. If current employees simply are not qualified, more extensive recruitment will be necessary. Current employees who apply for jobs and are subsequently turned down should be informed of the reasons for their deficiency and the improvements required. If this task is done with tact and in a positive manner, it can motivate employees to greater performance.

While promoting individual workers within the building company can prove beneficial, new employees will inevitably need to be hired from outside the organization on occasion. It is essential that these new employees have potential for growth. Planning for future needs is just as critical as planning for current needs. Too often, a building company will wait until a need is critical before giving much thought to hiring new employees; consequently, the company hires the first person available who is reasonably qualified, ignoring the long-term impact of this hurried decision.

Follow Effective Recruiting Practices. Recruiting potential employees is a skill that most superintendents need to develop and improve. A plywood sign at the construction site entrance is no longer sufficient—or desirable. Rather than being interrupted constantly by drive-by applicants who may or may not have the qualifications needed for the job, the smart superintendent develops an awareness of where the good prospects are and how to reach them. For example, you have contacts in the industry who can be of assistance in identifying qualified candidates. Other sources of potential employees include the following:

- everyday contacts on the job site
- subcontractors
- your file of potential candidates who applied for jobs earlier when no suitable position was available
- trade associations such as the National Association of Home Builders and Associated General Contractors
- educational institutes and schools
- material suppliers
- union offices
- building inspectors
- public employment offices
- private employment agencies
- advertisements
- competitors

Evaluate Application Forms and Resumes. Job applications are useful tools for assessing an applicant's qualifications. They contain information on the individual's experience and background, as well as data required for recordkeeping purposes.

While resumes are almost unheard of in the construction industry, a resume should be requested of all applicants applying for management positions or other positions of significant responsibility within the organization. A resume can provide you with a concise statement of the applicant's education, work history, and other related experience. The resume also helps to demonstrate the applicant's communication skills.

Conduct the Initial Screening and Interviews. Once all the necessary information has been gathered, you should review the information carefully and conduct the initial screening, weeding out candidates who are obviously unqualified. This screening should result in a list of potentially qualified candidates to be interviewed.

While effective interviewing is the key to successful hiring, it is a skill few people have developed sufficiently. You will find it well worth your time to develop interviewing techniques. These techniques will help you to both assess each candidate's qualities and qualifications and provide each candidate with information about the job. While assessing candidates will be your primary concern, the latter responsibility should not be neglected; you want to provide sufficient data to allow the candidate to make a reasoned decision about joining your organization.

You should prepare for every interview and set the stage for it. Before your first interview, determine what information is needed from applicants. This preliminary planning should result in a list of questions for all candidates. In addition, your pre-interview preparation for each candidate should include a list of additional questions appropriate for each individual candidate. As an effective interviewer, you should also review each candidate's work history to determine any unclear points and to avoid asking candidates to restate information already covered in an application or resume.

To achieve good results, candidates must be made to feel at ease, and a casual atmosphere will help. You should not try to place the candidate in an inferior position by sitting behind a desk, but rather in two chairs facing each other in an informal setting. Make certain that you are not interrupted during an interview. In addition, good interviewers always try to follow the following guidelines:

- Allow sufficient time for the interview.
- Be systematic and organized.
- Rate all candidates on the same criteria.
- Stick to the schedule.
- Allow time between interviews to evaluate candidates and prepare for the next interview.
- Do not oversell the organization or the job.
- Avoid leading questions such as, "You like hard work, don't you?"
- Be fair. Do not discriminate.
- Give candidates all the information required to make a decision.
- Be personable, friendly, and considerate.

Check References. References should be requested of all job candidates. While they can sometimes be biased, they can be a good indication of where to look for additional, more objective information. If an applicant is a recent high school, trade school, or college student, you may find a transcript of credits helpful. You may even want to do a little digging to uncover previous jobs that a candidate has not listed on an application or resume; contacting these employers or clients may provide much useful information.

Checking candidate references will allow you to better judge each candidate's personal characteristics. Therefore, put most of your efforts into assessing the candidate's compatibility with former co-workers, employers, teachers, and others. A history of jumping from job to job should be checked carefully to determine the real reasons for the moves. Thorough reference-checking should reasonably determine if a candidate has a problem getting along with people or following through on commitments.

Conduct Final Interviews. Occasionally, final interviews with top candidates will be necessary. Many builders and superintendents prefer to conduct these informal interviews outside the office, taking the candidate to jobs currently in progress. The ride time can be used to explain company goals and describe the position in detail. Problems pertinent to the new employee are explained. You may even ask the candidate to react to these problems and offer suggestions for possible solutions.

At some point during the final interview, you should provide each candidate with a detailed job description explaining exactly what the duties are and anticipated interaction with other employees. You may also want to introduce candidates to those with whom they will be working directly, if possible. If you will not be the future employee's immediate supervisor, that supervisor should thoroughly examine all top candidates as well and be given the responsibility and authority to make the final decision.

Make a Final Selection. At this stage, you should be familiar with the top candidate's attributes, abilities, and qualifications and be prepared to make a final decision. As emphasized at the start of this section, this decision to hire should be based on the company's needs and an applicant's ability to meet these needs.

Once you have made your decision, make an offer. Occasionally, superintendents and builders who have done a good job in the selection process make a tragic mistake at the last minute that may cause the entire process to fail: they try to get the person they want as cheaply as possible. They believe—usually mistakenly—that by keeping the price low, they can always bargain and raise the price later. Unfortunately, this practice can do a great deal more harm than good. Instead of the employee coming to work with a positive attitude and feeling good about the company, the employee may become suspicious and work below potential. Essentially, the old adage "You get what you pay for" holds true in this case. High quality personnel is the single biggest investment a building company can make. The more invested in personnel, the more returned.

Fringe benefits, such as sick leave, vacation, insurance, and use of company vehicles can be just as important as salary. Several studies have attempted to determine the relative importance of various means of compensation. Almost without exception, salary was not at the top of the list in any of these studies, but fourth or fifth after proper recognition, opportunity for growth, good working atmosphere, and opportunity to use skills and knowledge.

Training Hired Personnel

Once the right person has been hired for the job, you will need to turn your attention to training the new employee. Since the superintendent is responsible for training the field staff in new, more effective methods of construction, training and education are important keys to your success. They can make the difference between a growing, dynamic building company and a stagnating, declining one.

Training employees has several important advantages:

- Training improves job performance.
- Employees take pride in a company that devotes the time and money necessary to train its employees.
- Training is a two-way process. The "I care" attitude created often improves communication, which, in turn, encourages suggestions from employees that may improve performance.
- Training in safety procedures and methods reduces hazards and improves a company's safety record.
- The superintendent can train employees in the best and most economical ways to perform certain jobs, giving the company a competitive advantage.

Induction. Induction is the first important step in training a new employee. Effective induction procedures for each new employee can establish a positive attitude toward the new work environment for some time to come. During this initial period, the worker either confirms or changes his or her expectations of the building company.

Almost every job in a building company can be done many different ways, many of which are correct. New employees are often apprehensive about the way they have been taught and will probably take several days to adjust to changes in their new work environment. One means of easing this initially awkward period is to assign a particularly personable employee to work closely with the new employee for a few days to answer questions and help the new person adjust.

Orientation. Orientation is the next step, a time when the new employee becomes comfortable with the work environment. New employees are commonly concerned with the following during the orientation period:

- relationships with others in the organization
- tools and equipment policies
- payroll and timecard policies
- quantity and quality standards
- rules and regulations for conduct on the job
- involvement in apprenticeship programs (if applicable)
- advancement

Most of these concerns can and should be handled in a company policies and procedures manual. Unfortunately, many smaller building companies—and even some larger ones—have not developed these manuals. Superintendents and builders should therefore work together to create a company manual that helps each new employee answer six basic questions:

1. What is my present position?
2. What are my responsibilities?
3. What are my rights?
4. What limitations do I have?
5. Where can I go from here?
6. Where do I go when I have a problem?

Training Methods. Several methods are available to improve new and current employees' knowledge, skills, and attitude:

- *Apprenticeship programs*: These programs, lasting from one to five years, are the traditional means of training tradespersons. By rotating from one operation to another and receiving related technical instruction, apprentices acquire additional skills, master the application of those already learned with speed and accuracy, and develop independent judgment. This training method enables these individuals to be productive throughout the training period.

Studies have shown that workers completing an apprenticeship are more highly trained, work more steadily, learn new jobs faster, and are more likely to be supervisors than workers trained in other ways.

- *On-the-job training programs*: These programs have proven successful for many building companies. Similar to traditional apprenticeship programs in many respects, on-the-job training rotates employees from job to job, giving them a broad background in various aspects of the building business. Experienced workers are often used to teach employees the necessary on-the-job skills.

- *Planned work activities*: Planned work activities can be an effective training method for specialized jobs. For example, carpenters and supervisors from an experienced crew can be asked to train workers in the more effective techniques used in wood-frame construction. This type of training can eliminate much of the expensive trial-and-error learning too common in the building industry.

- *Individual instruction*: On occasion, individual instruction may be necessary to teach a worker a particular task on a one-on-one basis. The training steps offered in Figure 19 may prove helpful.

Figure 19: How to instruct

1. Prepare the trainee
2. Put the trainee at ease
   a. Introduce yourself to the trainee
   b. Get acquainted
   c. Show the trainee the whole job
3. Eliminate fears
   a. Assure trainee that he or she can learn the job
   b. Stress the importance of following and completing every instruction
4. Focus attention
5. Find out what the trainee already knows about the job
6. Select the one idea that offers the best starting point
7. Maintain the trainee's interest in the job
8. Explain what the trainee will gain (skill, knowledge, etc.)
9. Spell out any ground rules
10. Explain the need to ask questions
11. Describe the format of the training
12. Present the key points of the lesson
13. Demonstrate and explain
14. Have the trainee do the job
15. Ask questions and encourage the trainee to ask questions
16. Review procedures and routines

7

Working with the Buyer

Introduction

As a construction superintendent, you will spend much of your time on the job site supervising the construction process. However, the fact remains that you also play an important role in customer satisfaction, in helping buyers achieve the "American Dream" of home ownership. Therefore, it is essential that you understand home buyers and their needs in order to meet those needs effectively and profitably.

Understanding Home Buyers

While it may seem a little odd to some, most home buyers consider their homes an outward extension of all their hopes and dreams. Anything short of their mental picture of the perfect home can be devastating. The buyer probably breezed into the sales office loaded with ideas fueled by magazines. These publications were likely full of glossy photo spreads of million-dollar homes and articles telling home buyers how to deal with builders and get the most for their money. While some of the buyer's ideas may have merit and others may not, the buyer may refuse to listen to reason or discuss a point rationally. Recognizing that a new home is usually the largest single purchase most people ever make may help you to understand what might otherwise be viewed as strange or erratic behavior on the part of the buyer. Try to look at a given situation through the eyes of the buyer to better understand motives and avoid potential problems.

The Superintendent's Role in Customer Satisfaction

Your main goal as a superintendent is to maximize the company's profit in the long term. Earlier chapters have discussed how bringing the job in on time, within the budget, and according to the quality required is essential to achieving this goal. However, a superintendent who does all of the above yet fails to deal effectively with home buyers is not maximizing profits in the long term.

Why? It has been said that the greatest asset a construction company can have is a good reputation. Happy, satisfied buyers will spread the word, and the two largest factors in buyer satisfaction are the quality of the work and *the way they were treated*. A third, related factor that can affect all areas of buyer satisfaction is time. For example, you may often find that the buyers of a house that falls behind schedule are more difficult to please in terms of workmanship. Likewise, if the house is ahead of schedule, buyers may be more willing to overlook minor deficiencies. Keep in mind that many buyers feel that they are buying not only a new home but a large dose of personal attention. Providing this attention within reasonable limits can smooth relations with buyers considerably.

Post-Sale Letdown

Every superintendent should keep in mind that a certain degree of "post-sale letdown" is common after any purchase, particularly one as large as a new home. A buyer suffering from this letdown usually has the feeling that perhaps he or she made a bad deal. While it may seem like a job for the sales staff, you must do your part as a superintendent to reduce the symptoms of post-sale letdown. You can help by reassuring buyers of the wisdom of their decision. Simple statements such as "You're going to love living in this house" or "This is a great neighborhood" often help buyers reach the conclusion that perhaps their decision was a good one after all.

Policies and Procedures

Customer service policies and procedures will normally be largely dependent upon the contractual relationship existing between builder and buyer. For example, a job performed under a lump sum or fixed price contract puts you in more of an "arm's-length" relationship with the buyer than a cost-plus contracted job. With the latter, the buyer deserves to know not only the cost of different items of work but also *why* certain procedures are being used. Another primary factor to consider is whether or not an architect is involved and to what degree. If an architect is involved, he or she can be enlisted to help in answering a buyer's questions and explaining construction procedures.

Increasing Buyer Understanding

One essential policy should insist that all buyers understand exactly what they are buying. For example, buyers often have difficulty managing the leap from construction drawings to an actual house. By showing comparable room sizes, layouts, and details, you can enhance the buyer's awareness of the true finished product. Perhaps even more important than these items is an understanding of the quality of finishes to be expected. If the buyer was shown a model or other sample home, you must ensure that the buyer's home meets or exceeds the model in every respect.

Example: Buyer X. Some buyers, unfortunately, will remain unsatisfied even when the home meets or exceeds the quality of the model. For example, Buyer X had sold his first home and was moving up to his dream home. He had seen examples of the builder's finished product and was satisfied. One night, after his house was completed, Buyer X held a spotlight up against the walls and marked each and every imperfection. In addition, he complained that the tops of the door casing in one of the closets had only one coat of paint. While the builder agreed to try to fix the drywall imperfections, he explained to Buyer X that these imperfections would not be noticeable under ordinary lighting conditions. To prove the point, the builder took Buyer X and his spotlight back to the home Buyer X had lived in for years and showed him large imperfections that had earlier gone unnoticed. In addition, an inspection of the tops of the door casing in the closets revealed not only the absence of a second coat of paint, but the absence of any paint at all.

Obviously, handling extreme cases like this one with tact and understanding can prove difficult at best, but the dividends can be great. You must always remember that you are a professional and conduct your superintendent duties in a professional manner at all times. By doing so, you can often turn a potentially bad situation into one that enhances your company's long-term reputation.

The Importance of Contracts. When dealing with home buyers, whether in relation to a custom home, semi-custom home, or completely speculative home, there is no substitute for a good contract, one that touches all the bases and is easy to understand. Buyers naturally fear "snake oil deals" and contracts with the proverbial "small print." A good builder or superintendent will take to time to make certain the buyer understands everything in an agreement.

Buyer-Requested Changes. An important area to discuss with every buyer, and include in every contract, is the policy regarding changes to the work. If an architect is involved, the architect's understanding of change orders should smooth the process considerably. In any event, two things must be made clear regarding changes:

- One person will authorize changes on behalf of the company.
- All changes will be written and will include an exact description of the change, the difference in the sales price, and the change in schedule, if any.

This policy is especially important to follow on cost-plus homes. In a recent court case in Maryland,* a builder failed to keep the buyer up-to-date on cost overruns on a cost-plus job. The builder subsequently had to absorb these overruns because he failed to keep up with them in an orderly fashion and keep the buyer informed. The court ruled that cost-plus jobs are different from ordinary fixed-price contracts in that the builder owes the buyer a duty to act in the buyer's best interests. Therefore, the builder was obliged to keep up with the overruns so that the buyer could make appropriate adjustments as required.

Buyer Visits and Company Contacts. Some construction companies have policies stipulating when buyers may visit the job site. Some companies also pair each buyer with a contact person within the company to answer any questions that may arise. With most buyers, such procedures are unnecessary. However, a buyer will occasionally come along who is on the job site constantly, asking

---

* Jones v. J. H. Hiser Construction Company, Inc., 484 A.2d 302.

questions of everyone. Such buyers are usually just showing a keen interest and curiosity and do not realize that their presence is disruptive to the normal job rhythm. In certain cases, you will have to make buyers aware—in a tactful manner—that the builder is not trying to hide anything or get away with shoddy workmanship or substandard materials. Explain that in order for the job to flow smoothly, job site visits must be at preappointed times, and questions must be channeled through one person. This contact person may be the superintendent or someone on the sales staff.

Conflict Resolution

Conflicts arise among the various parties on construction projects practically every day. By virtue of your position as the superintendent, you are called upon to arbitrate many of these disputes. For example, if one subcontractor has damaged the work of another, it is up to you to assess proper back-charges.

Disputes with buyers are somewhat different in that the superintendent has a greater vested interest in the outcome. You will find that establishing and following procedures, particularly the types of procedures discussed in this book, are the easiest ways to avoid or settle these disputes.

Handling Buyer Conflicts

When you find yourself involved in a conflict with a home buyer, both parties must be encouraged to keep their heads and act in a professional manner. First, both parties should state their positions in clear and simple terms, giving all the reasons or justifications for their positions. You must then evaluate both positions in a fair-minded way. If you determine that the buyer is right, this should be admitted and appropriate action taken. However, you must remember that a fine line exists between exercising the golden rule and giving away the store. Admissions of responsibility or liability made by a superintendent in a spirit of appeasement are often used later in the courtroom to win an otherwise weak case.

If the buyer's position is weak or based on faulty reasoning, you should tactfully point out the fallacies in the buyer's argument. Take care to use thoughtful words in these instances in an effort to smooth an already sensitive situation. Cramming something down a buyer's throat may give the superintendent some momentary emotional satisfaction, but this action has a price that is usually paid for with a decrease in goodwill and reputation.

Daily Job Log. Many superintendents keep a daily job log or diary. Conflicts and resolutions should be entered religiously, since notes made at the time of the occurrence carry a great deal more weight in the unhappy event that you end up in court.

After the Sale

After the sale is another critical time in a customer service program. The superintendent will be required to service warranties, call-backs, and punch lists in an organized fashion that enhances—rather than diminishes—customer goodwill. The customer's demands will not always coincide with builder policy. However, effective, common-sense procedures, combined with tact, good listening skills, and a willingness to please, can go a long way toward eliminating much of the disagreement common in post-sale customer service work.

Scheduling Customer Service Calls. Random, spur-of-the-moment customer service calls waste time and money. If you are given the responsibility of handling customer service calls, you should arrange to have them scheduled on a regular, manageable time table. This scheduling procedure should be in writing and should be made clear to all buyers—either by sales and customer service staff or by the superintendent.

This type of scheduled customer service is usually based on two scheduled after-sale service calls: one at 30-60 days and another after one year. Buyers are asked to keep a record of minor problems for correction at these regular intervals. Many companies increase buyer goodwill by conducting these call-backs even when there are no obvious repairs to perform, dropping by simply to answer questions and explain any unclear operating procedures. Of course, emergency service should be provided immediately on an as-needed basis.

Subcontractors and Customer Service. If your company is small, you will probably depend on your subcontractors for much of your service work. Good communications and effective record-keeping are your first lines of defense in ensuring timely, quality customer service work from subs. Do not shift a customer's complaint to a subcontractor just to get rid of it, but do direct service calls to the proper subcontractor when appropriate. Your company may wish to consider using standardized four-part forms to write up work orders for subcontractor call-backs. You should keep one copy and give the rest to the sub; upon work completion, one copy remains with the sub, one copy with the customer, and one copy back to you (or the customer service office, if applicable).

Keep in mind that prompt attention to service requests is a key component of good customer service. Remember, the customer doesn't care *who* does the work, only that it gets done—properly and quickly. You may therefore wish to form an agreement with your subs that asks them to assign certain days or hours of days to perform call-back work.

Warranty Service Voucher System. Many building companies offer their customers a special voucher system that provides for callback service while providing an incentive for customers to perform their own small repairs rather than request service callbacks. Such a system begins with an account opened in the name of the buyer for a pre-determined amount, such as $200. Special vouchers are then given to the buyer, each worth $20, for use in requesting service. Service work is then paid for with the vouchers, and any funds remaining in the account at the end of the warranty period are returned to the buyer, with interest. These programs have proven extremely successful and may prove effective in your company if carefully managed.

8

A Final Word

Residential building is one of today's most exciting and challenging businesses, and one in which the construction superintendent plays a large and important role. The feeling that comes from successfully organizing people, materials, and equipment to create a beautiful and functional home can be quite special. When you pass a home that you helped to build years earlier, you probably find it difficult not to look at it with at least a small sense of pride and think, "I built that!"

This pride is at the heart of true success in the construction business. The truly successful are often not those who are wealthy or brilliant, but those who are genuinely good at what they do and take pleasure in it. In turn, most people who are good at what they do apply simple rules and goals to their tasks. This book has attempted to present such simple rules, targeted at budget, schedule, and quality, that can lead to maximum profits—and maximum superintendent success—in the long term.